ENTANGLEMENT

Library of Congress Cataloging-in-Publication Data

Entanglement
Alethea Pascascio
        p. cm.

ISBN: 978-0-9778377-2-4

1. Erotic Fiction. 2. Women-Drama. 3. Forgiveness-

LCCN: 2020924660

Publisher: Queen Publications

P.O. Box 4

Lansing, IL 60438

Dedication

This book is "both dedicated to the faithful and presented to the false-hearted to encourage the renewal of temperance and virtue."

-Introductory message of Cheaters syndicated television program

Acknowledgement

Heavenly Father, thank you for your grace and mercy.

I must acknowledge and thank my mother, Margaret Sherls (Ray) for standing in the gap for me while I worked at my laptop for an unimaginable number of hours. Your love and support are priceless. I love you greatly. My younger children, Alaina and Shawn Jr, thank you for being patient with me when I was in my writing zone and needed a quiet space. Your love and understanding are unmatched, and I love you both endlessly. Alexis, my oldest child, I appreciate you reading and editing my first draft. Thank you for being one of my loudest cheerleaders during this project. I love you past the moon. My brother, Jermaine (Jaa), I so appreciate you having faith in me to do great things. Your words mean more than you know. I love you.

To my family; sisters & nieces, who helped ignite this project when it was just a mere idea. Your excitement was so encouraging: Juanita, Margie, Candi, Rinita, Cherrita and Kennie. Love you all.

And to my friends who were busy working on their own projects but still found the time to encourage me, thank you and I value you.

Carol Blakemore, thank you for helping edit the first draft of the manuscript as well. Your feedback proved to be quite valuable.

If I did not mention YOUR name, charge it to my head and not my heart. Thank you for every kind word, gesture, and conversation. Especially, the laughs. I love and appreciate you.

ENTANGLEMENT

Queen

Publications

Alethea Pascascio

CHAPTER ONE

Lights. Cameras. Glitter! Shouts of excitement rang through the crowd made up of fans and paparazzi which surrounded the red carpet being manned by well-built security guards with earbuds in their ears.

"Alexandria! Amir!" shouts came from the crowd.

The black power couple, holding hands posed on the red carpet as the flashes of lights flooded them, taking countless pictures that would make the entertainment news the following day. Amir Sheldon was dressed in a black tuxedo, which was a perfect fit for his well-built body, courtesy to years spent in the gym. His hair was neatly cut, but his beard was full and neatly trimmed. At 6'3, he towered over his wife, Alexandria.

Alexandria Sheldon had gone with a black glittery dress which clung to her curves like a second skin. With an open back revealing her smooth melanin, and a plunging cleavage in the front, she took "simple-sexy" to another level. Her hair was pulled back into a neat ponytail, with professionally done makeup and eye-popping lashes to accentuate the face that made her one of the beauties in Hollywood.

The bright lights reflected on the caramel complexioned couple, who stood out as the most powerful African American actor and actress. Amir's hand went around his wife's waist, earning a scream of excitement from mostly his female fans, who made up the bulk of his fanbase.

"Should we give them more?" Alexandria grinned, looking up at her husband although in her mind she wanted nothing more than space from him and to be free of this boredom.

Laughter bubbled in his eyes as his head lowered, his lips meeting hers. Sure enough, the crowd went crazy with a loud scream. Amir chuckled as their lips parted. That got them wild every time.

"I want you, Amir!" a woman cried, trying to make her way from behind the barrier, as she was stopped by two bodyguards.

"Let's head in," Alexandria said, holding her husband's arm.

Amir threw a wave as he headed into the event center where the Globe, a yearly award event was held. It was a celebration in Atlanta of African Americans' contributions to the arts.

The Sheldons made their way to the front of the hall, where they had their reserved seats. They made a few stops and exchanged pleasantries with friends and acquaintances. As Amir held a rather lengthy conversation, Alexandria continued on toward their seats.

"Alex! You are so damn hot in that dress! Where'd you get it from?" Regina said, hugging Alexandria.

"Thanks sweetie, you look amazing as well," Alexandria replied.

"Where'd you get it from?" Regina repeated.

"Leonardo Grey," she answered, referring to the luxurious Italian designer who considered her a muse.

"You got to hook me up with Leonardo. I wanna wear his dresses so bad, but he ain't taking my calls." Regina sighed as her eyes surveyed the nameplates on the tables near them. We're sitting next to each other!" Regina returned excitedly then beckoned to her husband, Philip. He was conversing with Amir while heading toward their seats.

"Great," Alex mumbled, with her signature smile in place. Regina continued to yap on, and Alex zoned her out. Regina was a cool person, and they had been friends for over three years, due to her husband's friendship with Amir, but she talked too much. By the end of the night, Alex was going to have a splitting headache.

"Regina, do you mind if I sit between your husband and my wife? Philip and I have a lot to talk about," Amir said.

Regina pouted, but she compiled, as Alex sighed in relief, flashing her husband a grateful look. He knew how much Regina's rants got to her.

The stage was abruptly luminated as their hosts, Amanda Blakes, a renowned newscaster, and Jimmy Jay, a rapper emerged. The crowd went into a loud applause.

The next hours flew by, with the audience entertained. There were cheers, laughter, and even the occasional boos. The performance from the musicians was enjoyable, except for that of Rit, a young rapper who almost masturbated on stage to everyone's disgust.

By the time the Sheldons received their awards and left the show, the fans had dwindled, although the paparazzi were still much alive.

"How does it feel to win the award for Best Actress of the year?" a reporter asked Alex.

"It is amazing!" Alex started. She had won three awards tonight, while Amir had won two. They had put in so much work into their movies. This involved months on set, days flying from one location to another, shooting in the early hours of the morning, and the after-production activities. Along with the earnings from their movies, it felt damn good to be appreciated for their efforts.

It took another thirty minutes of doing interviews before they were led to their chauffeured limo by security. As Alex settled into the backseat, she slipped out of her stiletto-healed Louboutins. Hell, a $1,200 shoe should have felt like clouds on her feet but they had been killing her baby toes all night. She moaned in delight as Amir lifted her feet, and used his tender hands to massage them. The man's fingers could be a delight.

"I don't think I'm going to the Essence awards next weekend," Alex said. In the past weeks, she had hopped from one event to another, and finally needed a break.

Amir chuckled. "You do recall we are presenting an award together."

Alex groaned. As a celebrity, it was expected that she loved the glitz and glamour, and she did love it, but sometimes it got so tiring. She would prefer to lay in bed all day, binge watch a reality show, or just stroll on a private beach, but living the glamorous life came with its responsibilities, which could be a burden.

"Tonight was a win for us," Amir said, with a satisfied win.

"When has it never been?" Alex asked. Together, they had countless awards and recognitions by various national and international bodies, and they were still counting.

Both, age forty-five with a few months apart, the couple had begun acting in their early twenties. Amir initially had not wanted to be an actor, but at twenty-three he had been out of college, broke, and unemployed with a degree he realized too late was a waste of years in college. Amir had followed a friend to an audition, and had decided at last minute to try out. That had been his first acting job, a few scenes in a high school movie which had gone straight to DVD with low earnings and ratings. A few months later, he received a call with good news from a fellow cast member who had bonded with Amir during the production. That movie had seized the attention of a few Hollywood executives and eventually made its way into the cinema, and had opened the doors of stardom to Amir.

Alexandria on the other hand had always wanted to be an actress. Growing up in a Christian home, she had showcased her talents in dramas in the church, where she usually played the leading role. In high school, her love for the stage continued as she joined the drama team, where she became the face of the team, earning applause when the curtain fell. Her parents however had wanted her to be something more, away from acting which seemed sinful; they had pressured her into choosing a major in accounting.

However, while in college, Alex had several friends in dramatic arts, and soon she was acting in the college drama club. She had also participated in movies and documentaries directed by friends mostly for free or for lunch. After college, while working at a taxation company owned by a deacon at the church, Alex had started attending drama classes. One morning, while prepping for work, she stared in the mirror and said "enough is enough". There would be no more living her life unfulfilled and going to that mundane job. Alex threw caution to the wind and decided it was time to follow her heart. She packed up her vehicle and decided to drive from Florida to Atlanta to make a name for herself.

The car stopped in front of their Buckhead estate's wrought iron gates, and the window rolled down so the chauffeur could punch the password into the security keypad. The gates opened allowing the car to drive in past an aisle of trees. It went around a sprouting water fountain, stopping in front of a white huge multi-storied building. Three years ago, the house which sat on five acres had been bought for $22 million. It housed seven bedrooms with en-suite bathrooms, two living rooms, an industrial sized kitchen, an Olympic-sized pool, a basketball and tennis court, a 20-seat theater, a stable, and six car garage. Despite having penthouses in several states including California, this was home.

"Thank you, Rio. I hope you had as much fun as we did," Amir said, helping his wife out of the car.

Rio chuckled. In his sixties, he was a former Navy Seal, who looked innocent with his kind eyes and lean body, but Amir had seen him in action a few years ago when a stalker had hidden in his car. He was not one to be played with.

The front door opened as Alexandria typed the code into the keypad. She sighed in pleasure as she walked into the foyer. She loved their home no doubt, but at times it seemed just too big. They didn't have live-in help because of their privacy, but daily, the staff came in to clean the house and attend to their needs then left in the evening. Security was tight as there was a security system with motion-sensored cameras all over the grounds. In all their years of living here, they had never had one break-in or an intruder.

"Regina was right, you look great in that gown," Amir said, his hands around his wife's waist, pulling her to him. Alexandria moaned as his kisses peppered her neck. He knew how much that made her weak.

"Take it off me," Alex said, right before running up the stairs to their bedroom.

"I'm coming for you!" Amir yelled, struggling to get off his tie. Hell, he was filled with the excitement of the night. The performances. Meeting old friends and competitors. Winning awards that would soon line his shelf. And to end the day with such a perfect woman. He was one lucky man!

Amir sighed in disappointment when he walked into the room. Alexandria had taken the dress off without his help. He stared at her, basking in her near-nakedness. The woman was freaking hot! She had on a black matching underwear, the bra barely covered her firm breasts, and he could see the hardness of her nipples. His eyes drifted down as his dick hardened. He wanted to rip that thong off, the thong which wrapped around her gorgeous and firm ass.

"Are you gonna keep looking at me or what?" Alex smiled. She knew that look in his eyes. He wanted her.

Amir pushed his jacket to the ground and shrugged out of his shirt, revealing abs that made her pussy wince in delight. Then with quick strides, he got to her, pulling her to him. Their lips met in a firm kiss. Alex moaned as his hands swiftly discarded her panties then bra, her breasts crushing against his chest. He guided her to the bed, positioned her body with legs spread wide then slid his tongue into her tasting her juices. Her heightened moan caused him to retreat a little then French kiss her clitoris. Alex felt her inferno on the brink of an explosion. Her legs almost intuitively wrapped her husband.

"Amir! Amir! I'm I'm cuuumin." Alexandria wailed as his lips pulled away from her. She clenched the sheets as he rose and kissed her neck, then going lower until he stopped at her breasts which stood erect. Her eyes closed as his hot mouth pulled one of her nipples in, sucking softly on her. "Oh my goodness!" Alex cried, as her legs pulled together. She wanted him inside of her. Now! She reached for his belt, and quickly unzipped him as his rod sprung out.

Amir groaned as her soft hands gently stroked his erection. He was going to cum if she kept doing that. Laying between Alex's legs, he toyed with her juices then slid a finger inside. He groaned. She was an ocean! It never ceased to amaze him how ready she always was.

"I need you... I need you..." He thrust into her with a groan.

Alex gasped as he began to sex her, thrusting into her, and then pulling out. Her hands went around him as she tried to pull him in deeper. She wanted to feel all of him. And it was at that moment, it went downhill. With a muffled yelp, Amir came in her after only five pumps, flooding her with his hot cum. He continued stroking her, but she felt uncomfortable with his limp dick. So to move the experience along, Alex clenched her legs around him tighter and feigned her way through it. She let out a fake scream as her face contorted into what she believed was a good orgasm face.

"Was that okay?" Amir asked with concern as he pulled away from her.

Alex patted his face with a smile. "Yes, it was babe. I need to take a shower," she said as she slid off the bed.

The huge bathroom had dark grey marble floor tiles, and a huge gold-plated bathtub which Alex loved to soak in, but not tonight. She headed for the shower. Hot water ran down her skin as she washed off with a lavender-scented soap. The water was still running, when she grabbed the shower head. She set it at the highest and targeted it on her clit. Alex bit her lips as the hard force of the water hit her.

She pulled it closer and closer and almost stumbled before using her other hand to hold on to the wall. Her eyes on the door, she continued to take deep breath and low gasps. Her eyes shut for an instant as the beautiful and weak feeling overwhelmed her.

Alex emerged from the shower, and swaddled her body with a white fluffy bath sheet that she had gotten during a shoot in Saudi Arabia. She stood in front of the mirror, staring at her now makeup-free face. She loved makeup, but also loved herself without makeup. Thanks to good genes in her family, she had always had acne-free skin. While others her age had struggled with skin problems, all Alex did was put on mascara and a lip gloss then be on her way. Years later, she still was that way. At 45, she looked ten years younger with her non-blemished skin. She had also taken advantage of skincare products and procedures such as regular facials in her younger years, and paid for it now with her glowing skin. She didn't have eyebags, and barely had any sagging.

It was not just Alex's face. Her entire body was this way. Youthful. Her boobs were firm and round, and her stomach flat and toned. She was curvy, but not fat, and looked damn hot in anything she had on, making her the ideal recipient of various clothing from both known and unknown brands. Black indeed did not crack.

Despite her acting skills, her face and body were a market, and this was why it always irked her to see younger women fool around with their bodies. BBL, liposuction, botox, etc. These women were going overboard with cosmetic procedures. The other day she had been on set, and a new actress in the industry, in her early twenties walks in. That plastic ass had been so obvious from the moment she crossed the threshold. It was a hell no for her! These young bitches were trying too hard. They failed to realize that the foundation is laid in their youth. By the time that young lady turns forty, she would look like a walking ad for plastic surgeons.

Thank goodness she had a supportive partner who lived healthy as well. Together they worked out, ate and lived a relatively benign life. It didn't mean they weren't flexible with their lifestyle, but they damn sure knew their priorities.

When Alex returned to the bedroom in a powder blue lace robe, Amir was fast asleep. She slid under the covers and cuddled next to him.

CHAPTER TWO

The aroma of freshly brewed coffee greeted Amir as he hurried downstairs, with his luggage bag which he placed in the hallway outside of the bedroom. He walked to the kitchen and watched his wife from the doorway prepare breakfast. They had people to do that job, but she loved cooking, and he loved eating her food.

"You gonna stare at me like a creep or grab a plate?" Alex asked without turning around.

Amir chuckled. He grabbed a mug and poured some coffee for himself. It was Kopi Luwak, an exotic brand which hit his nerves instantly. He needed that caffeine for the long day ahead.

A plate of bacon and eggs was placed in front of him and he grabbed a fork, spearing into his breakfast. He nodded in delight. As expected, it tasted great.

"So, when are you coming back?" Alex asked, settling opposite him at the table.

"Tuesday if shooting goes according to plan," Amir said. The director he was working with was known to waste time a lot, but he hoped the same would not be done this time around because they were working on a tight schedule and budget. "What are you gonna be doing?"

Alex had some events to attend, and a few lunch dates. She also had a meeting with a director who wanted her on a movie. "Just a couple of meetings, and I am meeting Fiona." Everyone in Hollywood knew who Fiona Richards was. For over two decades, she had served as managers to top players in Hollywood. She was known as

"The Manager". Anyone she managed became successful. There was just no freaking way about it. It didn't matter if the person had no talents, as long as he/she was on Fiona's client list, she worked damn hard to make them successful. If there was someone Alex could learn from, it was Fiona.

Being B list celebrities in Hollywood came with high demands. This involved several movie offers which meant busy schedules. As much as they tried to be present in each other's life, their schedules were taking a toll on them. Last year, for over three months Alex had been in Mexico shooting a movie, while Amir had been in South Africa for a biopic. They had made videocalls, and she had even gone to South Africa for a weekend, but they had seen such distance happen several times in others relationships, eventually causing a rift. The final blow had been when their closest friends, Justin and Naomi Hawkins, who had been married for twenty years with two children had ended their marriage. In their defense, the distance with them being on different coasts for almost a year had caused cracks in their marriage, with the realization that they needed a divorce.

Amir and Alex grew tired of splitting their time between California and Georgia. Georgia gave them a getaway from the hustle and bustle of the industry while still remaining connected to the many celebrities who had chosen the same arrangement. Georgia was definitely the better choice for a committed couple. It was hard work sustaining a marriage in Hollywood, worse when both partners were in showbiz. And then they began to ponder about not only the future of their marriage, but also their careers. And then, Amir had suggested that she give up her career.

At first, Alex had been furious. Why did she have to give up her career? Why not him? She had complained to her mother who had been honest with her. She was the woman. The wife. And it was her duty to build her home. Otherwise, it would collapse. Besides, Amir had not suggested she outrightly give up her career. He had suggested an alternative; that she become his manager.

Alex loved business. She managed their business and financial affairs. And she was always on the outlook for business opportunities for them. So, when Amir suggested her being his manager, and got the opportunity to think it over, it seemed like a good idea. She wasn't leaving acting abruptly. No. She was taking fewer roles while adjusting to her new career. She was also reaching out to renowned managers in Hollywood to learn from them. One of whom was Fiona who was excited to mentor her. While she would soon stop taking new roles, she would still play an active role in Hollywood, managing her husband who had a very good career.

Amir glanced at his wristwatch. He needed to be at the airport so he could fly out with the rest of the crew to Washington. He was starring in a thriller where he played the lead, a lawyer who was blacklisted by the big firms in the legal industry.

After breakfast, Alex walked him outside to where the car awaited. She hugged him, resting her head on his chest. Amir chuckled. She was such a baby. He was going to be gone for three weeks at most but still understood her reluctance. He had just returned from a few weeks on set and couldn't wait for her to be his manager so they could go everywhere together.

"Make sure you call when you get to Washington," Alex said, pulling away.

He handed his luggage to the chauffeur and reached for Alex, planting a kiss on her lips, allowing it to linger. That made him want to go back in, spread her legs and make love to her. A cough pulled them away. It was Rio, looking at them sheepishly.

"Mr. Sheldon, I apologize for the interruption, but we need to leave now," Rio said.

Hiding a laugh, Alex patted his chest. "Take good care of yourself."

As always, when the car pulled away from his waving wife, Amir felt some sort of emptiness in him. He couldn't wait to be back home in the arms of his wife. It was crazy how he had become this man. But should he be surprised? After all, this was what he had always wanted.

Growing up had made Amir always yearn for a traditional family, made up of a husband, wife and children. There was no option for divorce. None. Unlike Alex, who had grown up with siblings and her parents who were still married and had last year celebrated their 45th marriage anniversary, Amir had grown up in a dysfunctional home.

His parents had never been married, and he had spent his childhood bouncing from one parent's house to another in two different cities. He had also been a pawn in his parents' conflicts. Amir shook his head as he recalled how crazy it had been. They had fought all the time, physically and even in court, with the cops being called in several times. Even in their old age, his parents barely tolerated each other.

Amir wouldn't have minded their toxic relationship if he had a sibling, even a step-sibling, but after him, his parents had signed off having children, although he suspected his dad had some other children out there. Being an only child without siblings or cousins his age had sucked. He had to play by himself or his friends while at school. An introvert, he had few friends and spent his after-school hours with his head buried in books. It was not until high school when he joined the basketball team that he began to open up and make friends.

Amir had always wanted a large family, with a wife who would care for their several children. He had dreamt several times of walking into his house from work to be greeted by the warmth of soup in the kitchen, with his children seated around the kitchen table, and his wife wearing an apron. That had been his dream. Until he met Alex.

Amir had met Alex on the set of a movie, where they had played lead roles. The chemistry had been clear as day from the first time they set their eyes on each other. Hell, he couldn't stop checking out the black woman who had an air of confidence more than any one he had ever seen. And thought she was drop-dead gorgeous with none of the fakeness that many women had. Alexandria had been 100%

natural. Her lips, he had kept staring at them every time they were together in a scene. It was no surprise this distraction had caused several retakes. The director, Steven, had screamed at him and told him to stop wasting their time and to just invite Alex out to dinner. The whole crew had laughed, making him realize everyone could see through his bullshit. That night, he went out with Alex. It had turned out to be the best date of his life.

There was more to Alex than her beauty and body. The society was crazy now, with women having no regard for virtues. They were all over the TV and phone screens shaking their asses, and fighting with their fellow's baby mamas. What mattered to most of them was hair, designer bags, clothes, and bling. Amir knew this because he'd had his share of these women, who threw themselves at him when he was single, and still did even though they knew he was married. He'd had to dodge those gold diggers, and even had one of them try to force a pregnancy on him. That trickster played dumb the moment he asked her for a paternity test. It was damn crazy out there and he didn't pity any of his single friends because they had a lot of shit to put up with in order to get a good woman.

Alex was a breath of fresh air. She had been brought up with virtues of a Christian home and loved God. She was respectful and submissive, and treated her body as a holy entity. Despite being an actress, she had never been involved in any scandal. And yeah, everyone he had asked about Alex had good things to say of her. She was a sweetheart everyone loved. He had known from the first date that she was the one; the woman he was going to spend the rest of his life with.

Amir and Alex had gotten married after two months in a quiet but intimate celebration, attended by their family and friends. It was indeed quite a short time to get to know each other and get married, especially for someone who was so particular about having a true soulmate. But Alex had known she was the one, so why wait? He had been forty at the time, and had almost given up on finding the perfect woman. Amir definitely had his share of women, but he could not wife them because of the shortcomings that he refused to accommodate.

Five years later, and there were no regrets for asking her to be his wife. Together, they made a beautiful pair, an influence on the younger generation who seemed to have shunned marriage. Their marriage had also opened doors of opportunities for them, with more roles and endorsements. They were the ideal black power couple. Talented, wealthy, educated, and scandal-free.

The only hitch in their relationship, one he had always yearned for.. was children. Amir frowned as he relived the day Alex had told him she could not have children. Being a father was something he had always wanted. They never had sex with protection because they were both faithful, and Alex was not on any birth control, so he was definitely worried when in the third year of their marriage, she hadn't gotten pregnant. That is when he had suggested they go for a fertility consultation with the family doctor.

"Fertility consultation? I thought you knew," Alex said, turning around from the dishwasher where she was placing the dishes.

"Knew what?" Amir asked. He had already spoken to the doctor and inquired about openings the following week.

"That I can't have children," Alex continued with sadness.

Everything faded around him, completely going blank as his knees buckled beneath him.

Then, "Amir! Amir!!" Alex screeched helping her husband steady himself.

He drifted back into reality at his name being called. "You can't have children?" Amir asked, hoping he had heard incorrectly.

Alex nodded.

"What... what happened?" Amir hoped this was some joke, because he just couldn't fathom what the hell she was saying. He looked at her stomach, as if trying to see for himself why she couldn't have kids.

"Remember the accident I had in high school?" Alex asked.

Yes, she had told him about it. It had been a life changing event that had strengthened her relationship with God. Alex had been returning back from school when she was run over by a drunk truck driver. It was a miracle she had survived. For three months, she had been in the hospital. Although she had recovered without any major outward scarring, there were minor marks on her hips where an operation had been performed.

"My womb was destroyed during that accident," Alex said as she burst into tears.

He hurried over to her and embraced her as she cried. Damn! He was completely pissed at the asshole who had run her over. If he could lay his hands on that bastard, he would have made his life miserable.

"I didn't know that Alex. I didn't," he consoled. The news frustrated him. And for the next couple of days, he was distant, still dealing with the devastating news. Alex couldn't have children. This literally traumatized him to the point where he had to pull out of a movie production he had been casted for.

Amir had always wanted a little girl like Alex. He had imagined her pregnant, glowing as always, with a pregnancy bump. Heck, from the first week they met, he had imaginations of her caring for their children. And that dream had been ruined by some drunk asshole.

As much as he wanted to be pissed at Alex for not telling him about her inability to have children, firstly it wasn't her fault, and secondly, they hadn't talked about having children before getting married. There was a lot they hadn't known about each other before, and in the first year of their marriage, there was a lot to learn.

Dealing with the news that they couldn't have children had been difficult for Amir. Thank goodness he had not made the mistake of leaving her. He always said that when he got married, it was going to be once, and would last a lifetime. Although he wanted to be a father, he loved Alex, and they would find alternatives. And if there was none, life would go on. He had finally succumbed to the fact that they couldn't have it all.

CHAPTER THREE

A moan escaped Alex's lips as the vibrator brushed hard against her clit. Her legs tightened around it, pulling it further into her. Just as she began to climax, her phone began to ring. She let it ring, her orgasm a priority. As she came, the phone rang again. She glared at it then cleared her throat.

"Hello?" she snapped into the phone, without looking at the screen.

"Did I interrupt a meeting?" Amir asked.

"Oh. Amir. No, babe... I just... I... was doing some yoga," Alex said, taking deep breaths.

"Okay, I just wanted to let you know we're gonna wrap up sooner than expected, so Imma be home tomorrow. What you think of dinner at Diaz?" he asked, referring to a quiet restaurant.

"That would be great," Alex said.

"How was your meeting with Fiona?" Amir asked, as she stared at her vibrator. Just hearing his voice was making her horny again.

"Umm... it went well..." She thought of his thumb playing with her clit, as he sucked hard on her nipple.

"You okay?" Amir inquired.

"Yes, yes. I'm just... still breathless," Alex said, as she jammed the vibrator, now on low into her pussy. She hissed at the feeling. "How was shooting today?" she asked, as she increased the tempo.

"It was great, except for this kid. Joel," Amir hissed.

"Ooohh Joel, I heard he's an ass to work with," Alex said, her eyes shutting close as she held imagery of Amir ramming into her.

"That's an understatement. He's a fucking prick. Talk about entitlement and he's not even all of that. He ain't gonna last long," Amir confided.

She gasped at his words, coming in that moment. She held tight to the phone as the tremor passed through her body.

"You okay?" Amir asked.

"Sure, I am," Alex smiled. That was her fourth orgasm in less than an hour, and she was still horny.

"I got to go now. See you tomorrow hon," Amir said, right before the call ended.

Alexandria laid back on the bed, her naked body nestled in the 10,000 thread-count Egyptian sheets. She stared at the ceiling as her finger drifted lower, stopping in front of her dripping pussy. She wanted more. She wanted a shattering orgasm that would leave her weak for days. She chuckled at the thought because she knew her body would always crave for orgasms.

Alex had a high sex drive. She had realized it when she had sex at sixteen with the preacher's son who was in college. Drew was far more experienced and knew how to treat her well both in and out of bed. But he had left in her a certain hunger she had been scared of- both scared and embarrassed to reveal that she wanted to experience the raw nastiness of it all.

In college, Alex had a few boyfriends and although it had been a phase to experiment and learn what really turned her on, she still didn't feel the freedom to express her deepest sexual desires. She had wanted to be a tigress in bed, to ride on her boyfriend's penis then his face and climax over and over, but she had been scared of his reaction. Would he call her a slut? Those fears had kept her longings inhibited for many years causing her to take whatever was offered to her. Luckily, Amir was a caring partner who asked her what she wanted, and responded. However, Alexandria spared him her deepest desires, scared he would not be able to handle them, afraid she would no longer be on that pedestal in his eyes.

Men claimed to want a woman who knew her way in bed, but at the end of the day, they didn't want a woman who knew everything there was to know about sex or one who was willing to try anything. Such a woman was meant for the streets. At least that is what the older women at church taught her as a child about those "loose women".

It didn't help that Amir had insecurities. He was an absolutely gorgeous man, with a great body and decent dick. But in bed, he was worried about his performance. He would ask her several times if she was having fun, how many times she had orgasmed, and even told her to rate their sexual experience. Their sex life was good enough, but his insecurities and quick orgasms often put a damper on the moment. Also, it seemed like everything was routine, with no out of the box experiences. And he thought through his performance during sex, instead of letting it be organic and lead by passion. Not to mention, Alex had to massage his ego every time, even when she wanted to tell him the truth...she couldn't.

Imagine her telling him she wanted to ride his dick while she had a dildo in her ass, he was going to feel even more insecure, wondering where she had learned that from. She had thought about recommending a sex therapist, but suspected that would bruise his ego.

Most times, Alex had to take care of herself, but that wasn't enough anymore. She wanted more. She wanted the real deal, a fat dick ramming through her pussy walls. But she doubted she was going to get that with Amir, unless he could read her mind.

Cheating was not an option. Alexandria had come across deliciously handsome men in Hollywood who fucked her with their eyes, but she was married and had made a vow before God. She had never cheated on Amir, and would never. Alex knew it was the same on his part. He loved her too much to do that. She was lucky to have a man who loved her so much, and was willing to deal with her infertility even though he wanted a large family. An average sex life was a small price to pay.

Alex's phone rang just as she got out of the shower. It was her girlfriend, Kim. She and Kim had met in acting classes. They had started right at the bottom, hustling for the little acting jobs that had managed to come their way. However, Kim had given up on acting and went behind the scenes. She was now the CEO of a black-owned production company named, Black Diamond. She was one of her closest friends from way back.

"Girl! Where the hell are you?" Kim asked.

"Chill Kim, I am almost there," Alex smiled.

"Ha ha, you and I know your ass is still at home, wrapped up in a towel."

Alex laughed. "You damn right, but imma be there in twenty."

"Just bring your ass over here, I can't deal with Keisha's craziness alone."

An hour later and Alex walked into Spar, a luxury restaurant that catered mostly to celebrities. There were a few paparazzi outside, waiting to take pictures of the stars that entered. It could be quite frustrating. At times she just wanted to walk around like everybody else without being hounded by cameras. But it was the price to pay for being successful. Despite wanting privacy, she would choose this life over a drab one back in her hometown, probably married to a deacon, which was the life of most of her high school classmates.

Alex walked through the lobby, spotting some familiar faces and stopped by to exchange pleasantries. Then she headed towards their usual table which was on the patio.

"You made it at last," Trina said.

Over the years, Alex had made long-lasting friendships from production sets, collaborations, award ceremonies, auditions, etc. She couldn't even recall how some of the friendships had started. Most of her friends were Black or Latino, not for any particular reason other than those being the races that vibed with her the most.

Alex had met Trina during an audition twenty years ago. Neither of them had gotten the role but they had hung out that night and have been friends since then. Trina had gone back to her first love, medicine, and was on the board of various hospitals in Atlanta. She was married with three stunning kids.

Keisha was a frenemy. There were times Alex liked her, and times she just wanted her to shut up for good. Two failed marriages, she was now married to a big-time Atlanta Director who had revamped her career by helping her get quality roles. She was always in competition. If you said you spoke to Jaimie Fox, she will say she had lunch with Denzel. If your purse costed $2,000, her purse costed $5,000. It was never ending and there was nothing she didn't complain about. Hanging out with Keisha could be quite embarrassing as she had no filter.

Nancy was part black, part Latino. She was such a sweetheart, and could always be counted on. Alex was irked that Nancy's asshole of a husband had divorced her for some young little ass who spent his money shopping around all day. Nancy had gotten a hefty settlement, although the asshole husband found every opportunity to paint her name black in public. Perhaps that is the reason why Nancy starred only in TV shows.

The last at the table was Rita. Now, if there was anyone you had to call to bury a body, that was Rita. She had hustled her way to the top doing everything possible.

She had stripped, acted in porn, sold drugs, been an escort, and many other things that would traumatize the average person. She had finally struck gold with a sugar daddy, a wealthy millionaire who bankrolled movies. Rita got her first role where she acted as a call girl with so much flair, it got her several award nominations. She had dumped her sugar daddy and moved on to a wealthier one, who financed her luxurious life. Years later, she was married to that old man, and was a regular on Atlanta Wives, a reality show that focused on wealthy housewives in Atlanta. The audience knew Rita as no-nonsense who didn't allow others to mess with her family or friends. Her name always popped up in scandals, of her messing around with both men and women, and she didn't care to defend them. But I have to admit, inquiring minds want to know.

"Damn Miss Lady! You took forever, huh? I ordered you a long island ice tea." Rita asked as she filled her glass with champagne.

"I had a call with Amir which took some time," Alex said.

Alex knew the ladies wanted to talk about everything; sex, money, men, but personally she only confided in Kim and Rita whom she knew didn't have loose mouths. The others? While they might not have bad intentions, would run their mouths telling her business to anyone who would listen. If there was one thing she had learned in Hollywood- keep your damn business to yourself, otherwise it would end up in the tabloids.

"Awww... that's so sweet that your hubby called you. Ya know men, they're gonna call you to cover their tracks, so you won't know they're cheating," Keisha said.

"Come on Keisha! We all know Amir don't do shit like that," Trina scolded.

Keisha chuckled. "Men are the same. They're gonna screw any pussy they come across. Wouldn't even give a shit if they got a pregnant wife at home."

While Alex agreed there were trifling men, especially in Atlanta who screwed anything in skirts, Amir was different. He would not do anything to jeopardize their marriage. He was so consumed with making their marriage work, he wouldn't mess it up by cheating. Any man would have walked away three years ago when she told him she couldn't have children, but he had chalked it off, talking about alternate ways to have children.

"Amir is not like your husband, Keisha," Nancy threw, earning a glare from Keisha. Everyone knew Keisha's husband was a dog. He screwed actresses who were trying to make it in Hollywood with promises of roles. He had been involved in several scandals which had been hushed with money. But then Keisha had her own share of escapades, especially when it came to younger men.

"You're not gonna talk about my husband when you don't even have one!" Keisha threw back.

"Damn, girl!" Kim said.

That was definitely a low hit. They all knew Nancy's ex had been an asshole, and she had been a good wife to him.

"What? She started it first!" Keisha defended.

"No, you started it first with calling out Alex's husband," Rita said.

"I didn't call out anyone. I just said the truth. Just because you didn't catch your man in the wrong, doesn't mean he's not. You are not always there with him. Have you seen the bitches these days? At twenty they got big asses, and don't care around messing with your man then putting it on the Gram. Ain't no way he's not fucking those bitches. Your man is damn fine, and they're gonna be throwing themselves on him," Keisha continued.

She was right on the last part. Amir being married didn't stop women from wanting to fool around with him. She had received panties stained with cum in the mail several times, all addressed to him. He had to change his number several times because of the harassment from female fans, and only a tiny circle had his personal number. These bitches sent him nude pictures, including videos of them twerking and even masturbating. He had a private social media account, but his public account was managed mostly by his media manager who had witnessed countless messages and pictures from women who wanted to screw her husband. It was just so crazy out there. There was no limit for these women. However, Amir had never cheated. His heart beat for no other woman but her, and everyday she thanked God for sending her such a man.

"How's Theresa?" Alex asked, changing the topic. She wasn't going to argue with Keisha who always believed that she was right and had to win every argument.

"She's having her first lead role tomorrow," Nancy smiled. Theresa was her fifteen-year-old daughter who was so cute, and certainly going to be a star someday.

Trina sighed at the sight of the waiter. He was young, probably in his early twenties, and looked like a tall glass of chocolate. His well-built physique and broad shoulders were accentuated in his black and white uniform. His hair was packed in a dread ponytail, and the one earring in his left ear shined as much as his perfect set of teeth. He was damn fine, with a sculptured face. His eyes widened as he recognized the women at the table. They danced from one woman to another, until they rested on Alex.

"Hello ladies," he drawled in a sexy voice.

"Hi honey, what's on your menu?" Rita teased, leaning forward to reveal her cleavage.

"Anything you want," their waiter replied with a wink at Alex who shook her head amused.

"I will have the Salad and ribs," Kim said, in her no-nonsense voice, which wiped the flirting from his eyes.

"Umm… okay," he said, quickly writing it down. His smile returned as he took the order from Keisha, who didn't hide the fact that she liked him. "And you madam," he asked slowly, with a pointed look at Alex who was scrolling through her phone.

She looked up for a brief moment, then rattled out her order. "Get me the Zucchini salad, and I need a refill of my Long Island," Alex said.

"Is that all?" he asked expectantly.

"Yes."

They all watched his fine ass as he walked away, taking his time of course with the occasional look back.

"I want that ass," Keisha said.

This wasn't surprising. Keisha had a love for younger men, but she didn't pick them up in public places. Alex pitied the kid because Keisha was going to chew him up, and spit him out damaged.

"Too bad he got his eyes on Alex," Kim said, taking a sip from her glass.

"Yeah, that nigga wants to marinate you, wrap you up and eat the hell out of you," Rita said, earning a laugh from Nancy.

Alex giggled. Of course, she wasn't so naïve that she hadn't seen him flirting her way. She always seemed to draw the attention of mostly younger men, although there were the occasional older men too. However, they were more respectful towards her, than the women were towards Amir. Alex hardly ever received nude pictures and had never received a pair of boxers. Thank God they respected her that much.

"He needs someone like me with a little more experience. Besides, Alex isn't interested. You don't know what you are missing Alex. To fuck the same dick every day, girl I pity you," Keisha shook her head in sympathy.

"I gladly hand him over to you," Alex fanned her manicured fingers toward Keisha. There were hot men on the streets of Atlanta, and all over the world. Men hotter than her husband, and while she might have fantasies of fucking them, she would never cross that line to initiate such intimacy. Not only was that ruining her marriage vows, it was going to hurt Amir who trusted her. And it could damage her career if it got out in public. Alex knew the names she was called behind her back. Saint Alex. Miss Goody-two-shoes. Despite her good and responsible behavior, many were waiting for her to slip and make one mistake, so they could drag her through the streets of scandal. She wasn't going to give them the opportunity, but there were definitely times she wanted to throw all caution to the wind and let herself be free. Free in the worst kind of way.

Kim lifted her glass in a toast. "To fine young men."

Laughing, Alex joined in the toast. Indeed, to fine young men whom she could see and admire, but could never touch.

CHAPTER FOUR

Amir was home. Alex turned in the bed, as he settled next to her, his body fresh from the bath he had just gotten out of. He was supposed to have been home hours earlier but his flight had been delayed and she was too tired to wait up.

"Hey, love." Amir said, placing a kiss on her lips.

"Hey," she smiled at him through sleepy eyes.

"Ya miss me?" Amir asked reeking of his favorite cognac, Monte Blanc Reserve.

Alex loved when he took a shot of his favorite elixir. It heightened his sexual abilities and the aroma of it on his breath was a turn on to her, but she played coy anyway. "Hell no, I didn't miss you."

He chuckled. Well, he had certainly missed her, and was glad to be home. "You sure you didn't miss me?" he asked as he slowly lifted the bottom of her PJ's top.

"Amir," Alex complained. She'd had a busy day and really wanted some shut eye. Her resistance disappeared as his tongue circled her nipple.

He chuckled again after she gasped when he began to massage her other boob.

"I missed you so damn much," Amir said as he slipped his hands into her bottoms.

Alex wasn't wearing panties. She hated them, and only wore them when necessary. She moaned as he began to pump his fingers into her.

"Amirrrrrr," Alex cried as she grinded herself against him, silently begging him to add more fingers into her.

He pulled away from her and slipped her bottoms down, burying his head into her. Alex gasped as she tightened her legs around him, his tongue sliding into her wet folds.

"You taste so fucking good," Amir groaned, as his dick strained against his boxers. She moaned louder as her fingers dug into his scalp, her walls clenching around his tongue. She wanted more! She wanted him to slide his tongue deeper into her pussy until she exploded.

Right before Alex reached her climax, Amir turned her onto her side pressing her back against his front then gently lifted her leg. Her mouth widened as she felt his dick at her entrance. "I'm going to fuck you so good now," Amir whispered as his mouth nibbled at her shoulder.

"Yeaaaahhhhh," Alex hissed as he slowly slid into her pussy.

Amir managed to reach over and caress her pulsating clit while giving her slow strokes. That drove her crazy. Her scream was swallowed by his kiss as she climaxed, her body going limp as he shot his hot cum in her.

"I did miss you," Alex finally managed to say, curling up next to him, his arm around her waist.

"I know you did," Amir grinned.

"So how was the shoot?" Alex asked.

"Great. Production should be wrapped up in three months. We had a bit of a stalker who was taken away by the cops," Amir informed.

Alexandria had seen that in the news. Alfred, the director, had found a woman in his trailer, naked, and had gotten her arrested. It was alleged this was not the first occurrence, and he had let her off previous times.

"We will be having an extra plate at breakfast tomorrow," Amir yarned.

"Who?"

"His name is Jay Carlo," Amir answered.

Alex frowned. She had never heard of the name. "Isn't he like a baseball player?"

Amir laughed. That was the same thought he had had. Jay Carlo sounded like one of those Black Latino kids who played baseball. "Nah. He's the kid Brenda has been begging me to mentor. They stopped by on the set, and we talked for an hour or so. He's got potential."

In his way of giving back to the society, Amir from time to time mentored young actors. Despite his busy schedule, he worked with young talented minds whom he coached on acting techniques, and also helped with networking and getting roles. So far, he had mentored five actors, and all of them no longer struggled with roles as they did prior to meeting him. The most successful of his mentees was Richard Brown, who Amir had suggested for a role as a black superhero. The franchise had gone on to make over $400 million in cinemas alone.

Brenda was one of Amir's agents, whom he had worked with for the past decades. She had gotten him a lot of great roles and endorsements. However, Alex wasn't a fan of her. She really couldn't place the reason, but perhaps it had to do with Brenda coming off as someone who was willing to take shortcuts to get results, while Alex preferred the long and rewarding process. Alex was pretty sure that her and Brenda were going to clash when she became Amir's manager.

"I mean a lot of development needs to be done on his part, and he has a lot of growing up to do, but it is a favor for Brenda. Otherwise I would have gone with the Nelson kid," Amir continued. Nelson Froggs was eighteen and in Morehouse College, where Amir had some connections. His friend, a professor there, had recommended the kid for mentoring, and Amir had gone out to watch some of his plays. The kid was indeed talented and would go places. But Brenda had called him out on a favor, and although he was still going to work with Nelson, he was going to mentor Jay first. Amir could take on two mentees, but it would clash with his busy schedule – moreover, he liked focusing on one mentee at a time.

Albeit successful, he was a humble and down to earth. He was one of those actors whose fame hadn't gotten to his head, and like he always told his mentees who never took advantage of his kindness, his home was open to them.

Being a black male actor in a white dominated industry where racism and colorism thrived was difficult, and this was his way of helping to create a soft landing for those coming behind him. Amir often paid homage to the older actors who helped him snag his first acting gig, before they passed away, and that was his way of paying it forward to the next generation.

Amir was the first to wake up the following morning. He sat up in bed for a few minutes staring at his wife who slept peacefully. His heart warmed with love for her often wondering what he had done to deserve getting the best wife in the world. And he wasn't joking when he called her the best in the world. He had friends who were on their third marriages, and although they had a share of the blame, those women were bullshit to begin with. Some of them were gold diggers who spent all day shopping and travelling, and when they headed to court filed for millions in settlements which left the men broke. There were also the wives who liked to party and snorted coke like it was oxygen. Marriage in Hollywood and Atlanta was likened to a sham because of how easy it was to get married with a million dollar wedding, only to end a few months later, in a million dollar divorce lawsuit. He was one lucky man to have a responsible wife who worked her ass off, even though he could provide the life she wanted. She was one woman he could count on to be there for him, if he ever hit rock bottom. These women were hard to find. There were probably just ten of them in Atlanta, and he was married to one. It was why he cherished her so much. He would do anything for her. Anything!

"Stop looking at me like a creep," Alex mumbled, playfully swatting him.

"You fucking gorgeous you know?" Amir said.

A smile spread on her face at this. She loved when he complimented her, and he did a lot of that. Regardless of knowing that she was beautiful and hot, those words boosted her day and confidence.

"Time to work out," Amir said, just as the alarm went off.

They had a home gym with all the exercise equipment they needed, treadmill, barbells, dumbbells, etc. At times they worked out by themselves or their fitness trainer came around a few times during the week. They also had membership at a gym where they popped in once in a while.

Hours later, their bodies covered in sweat, they stepped into the shower. Alex had her breasts smashed to the tiles as Amir washed her back. Her eyes closed as his hands drifted lower with the soap. Her body froze as he ignored her ass, going lower to her legs. Every time he did that, walked away from her ass, she wanted to call his attention to it. She wanted him to play with her ass, to finger her there, to fuck her ass. Damn, she had so many fantasies featuring her ass, but since he never made any approach, she guessed he wasn't an ass man. And she didn't want him to croak at her fantasies.

Amir licked the droplets of water from her ear, his kisses getting slower as he went down her neck. Just as he began to really get into it, the phone rang from inside the room.

"Let it ring," Alex pleaded. She was feeling so good.

"It could be Jay," Amir said, as he regretfully pulled away.

"Who the fuck is Jay?" she cursed as he stepped out of the shower stall. Then she remembered, the new kid Amir was going to mentor. He had terrible timing!

Amir hurried to the room and caught the phone on the last ring. Sure enough it was Jay. "Hey Jay," Amir said.

"Did I call at the wrong time? We could reschedule our meeting, I am in an Uber right now, but I could turn around," Jay said.

He looked at the bedside clock. They were to meet over breakfast at nine. Working out had made them run late, and it was a few minutes to nine. "No, there's no need to reschedule. See you soon."

"Are you coming back?" Alex called, from within the shower.

"Jay's almost here!" Amir informed as jumped into his clothes still partially wet from the shower.

Alex rolled her eyes. She already could tell she was going to be in a tense mood until she had a date with her vibrator. Amir wasn't aware she had a sex toy, this would hurt his feelings and make him bring up his insecurities at their monthly meetings.

He was the one who had suggested the monthly happiness check in, to ensure that they were happy and meeting each other's needs and expectations. It was like talking to your shrink, only it was actually your partner. In his words, they had to be honest with each other, and bare it all out, so they could work on their marriage. Doing this, they would be accountable and work on their flaws. However, how could she tell him she needed their sex life to be improved? Or that at times she faked orgasms? She always assured him that he met her needs, despite his vocal insecurities that he feared he didn't. His ego was fragile, and she was not going to damage it more. Even if they weren't together, they had these meetings on video call. He was usually very open about what he felt, but she on the other hand held back. Alexandria just couldn't talk to him honestly when it would hurt his feelings. At times, someone had to be the sane one, and it seemed that was her. So she kept her toys tucked away, where she knew he would not find them, using them only when he was not home or somewhere else in the house.

"You okay in there?" Amir called as he grabbed his Rolex, swinging it around his wrist.

"Yes," Alex said, stepping out of the stall with a frown. When he went into his home office with the Jay kid, she was going to head back upstairs and continue with what he had stopped.

While Amir headed downstairs to ensure the chef was handling breakfast, she got dressed. She was not big on dressing fancy, except for award ceremonies, and even then, she was simple. She was not the celebrity you would spot on the red carpet with half of her vagina exposed. Nah, she was always a lady.

Alex's walk-in closet was hers alone, a huge closet, she had worked on with the interior designer. Amir had his own next to her, a smaller closet, which she had also helped design. She pulled out a T-shirt, then placed it back, settling on a black bodycon. She loved looking good, and looked damn good in the bodycon which of course stuck to all her curves like a second skin.

Ten years ago, Alex had started transitioning, deciding to go natural. She had a closet full of wigs, but her natural 4B hair was healthy and long, half-way to her waist when pressed out. She could switch it up whenever she wanted, just add some leave-in conditioner and left her fro free. While getting ready for her day, she heard a car pull up in front of the driveway. Amir's mentee was here. It always amused her when they seemed so excited to be in their home and their look of awe was priceless. If they played the right cards, they could have even more.

CHAPTER FIVE

The Uber driver gave a whistle of admiration, and Jay agreed with him.

"Damn man, how much this cost?" the driver asked as Jay stepped out.

Jay waved the driver off as he climbed up the stairs to the front door. He had always known meeting Amir would change his life, and this was made clearer as he was ushered into the foyer by the housekeeper. He looked overhead and his eyes widened at the gold chandelier that hung from above.

"Jay!"

Amir walked towards him, dressed in a black turtleneck and jeans. It still felt like a dream that he was up close with this legend, shaking his hand. He had watched him on the screens for over a decade, hoping to someday be like him. Now, he wanted to be better than him. The clothes he wore cost hundreds of dollars, like the sneakers he had on. Damn the man was almost fifty and he looked so good. Good dentition. Fit. Well-dressed. Power. Money. Sex. This was the life money and fame offered, and he wanted all of it.

"Your house is lit!" Jay said as Amir gave him a little tour. His new apartment which he would pay hundreds of dollars monthly for, leaving him damn near broke, could fit into the house ten times over!

Amir snickered. He enjoyed the gleam of excitement in the young man's face. And to think he had once been like him. Almost two decades ago, he had shared a miserable tiny apartment with three other dudes, all of them with dreams to be actors. He had been the only one to make it at being successful. Amir had been unable to bring a woman home; because of how tiny the apartment was the others would hear him making out. After that, he had shared a still small apartment but decent enough with Charles, who was now a bigshot agent. The climb to success had certainly not been an easy one. When he got a penthouse in downtown Atlanta, his first real home alone, he had stood in that penthouse looking all around in awe, thinking he had indeed made it. Years later, that penthouse was a tip of the iceberg.

"Like, this is so fucking dope!" Jay stood in front of the huge TV which dwarfed his 6-foot 3-inch frame. He and his homies had once gone to check out a TV with the same specifications and it was worth thousands of dollars. The quality from the TV was like that of a cinema.

"As an actor, you need the best TV," Amir joked. He had not done much with the designing of the house, that had been left to Alex who worked with the interior designer. However, he'd had a say when it came to the technology, wanting the best for himself. He freaking deserved it.

"I'm impressed," Jay said. This was an understatement. He was *freaking* impressed. But he knew better than to show that he was that excited. He didn't want to come off as being poor or thirsty. Better get yourself together, he warned himself. He had been to several parties at celebrity's homes, but this one did it for him. Millions had been spent on this home, and every piece was well selected.

"Let's go over to the patio, breakfast will be served there. Oh, there she is," Amir said, as Alex walked in.

Jay followed his gaze and for a moment, the world stopped revolving. He had seen her in movies. He had seen her on the magazines. Heck, he had seen her from a distance. But never this fucking close. Everyone knew she was gorgeous. Everyone knew she was hot. But seeing her in person, their praises for her were complete understatements. She was the most perfect woman he had ever seen. That radiating brown melanin. Those curves of hers. That pert mouth around his dick. Stop! He told himself. What the hell was he thinking.

"Alex, this is Jay, my new protégé," Amir introduced.

"Hello Jay," Alex waved.

However, Jay took her hand in his, and lowered his mouth, pressing a kiss that sent her entire body vibrating.

Alex quickly pulled away, wearing her signature smile. "Welcome to our home. How has Atlanta been to you?" She was impressed with how firm her words were, although she was shaking on the inside. Being in Atlanta meant she had come across beautiful men with gorgeous bodies. Jay wasn't number one on the list, but there was something about him that made her walls of resolute crack. She could tell instantly that he was trouble. He was taller than Amir, with smooth brown chocolate skin that she resisted running her fingers across. And he was so damn fine! With those hazel eyes that undressed her without any restraints. Alex knew he would fuck her right here if he could. He was fit, with firm arms and a well-toned body. Perhaps what made him more mesmerizing was his hair packed in a ponytail. She loved hair on a man. She imagined holding on to it as he thrusted his meat inside of her.

"Alex? Are you okay?" Amir asked. She looked kind of rattled.

"Umm… yeah," Alex said, recovering from her lust, as Amir pulled her to him, putting a hand around her waist.

"I am honored to be in the presence of the both of you," Jay said with sincerity.

He looked upon them with admiration and a hint of jealousy. They were the role models amongst black couples. So much in love, the couple got married two months after they met. How many years had they been married now? Seven? Nah, five, if his research was correct. It seemed like a lifetime compared to how short marriages were amongst celebrities, and theirs had remained scandal-free.

Amir chuckled. "Well, we are honored to have you here too. Right honey?" he asked, looking down at his wife.

Alex beamed a smile at her husband, as Jay watched her in a way that made her uncomfortable. It was like he was trying to read her, to unravel her every thought piece by piece, and this unnerved her. His gorgeous hazel eyes were just so damn calculative, she wondered what he was thinking. "Yes we are."

Jay grinned. He didn't buy the crap they portrayed. He had been around in Atlanta to know bullshit when he saw it. By the end of breakfast, he was going to know what the deal was with the couple, but by looking at Alex, he could already tell.

"I'm going to go check if breakfast is ready," Alex said, pulling away from her husband.

"Come on honey, help me give Jay some beginner's knowledge," Amir teased.

"I'm sure you have more than enough to give," Alex patted his chest. "I will leave you boys for now," she continued, hurrying away from Jay's penetrating gaze.

Alexandria almost collided with one of the maids as she walked into the corridor, hurrying off as the maid called an apology to her. She stopped running when she got to her bedroom, shutting the door and slipping to the ground. It was then she realized her hands were shaking.

In all her years, she had never been badly affected by a man as she had by Jay. This was crazy! She laughed hysterically. Hell no! How old was the kid again? Twenty? He was way too young for her to mess around with. Why would she even think of messing around with him in the first place? There's no way she was going to cheat on Amir. It had never happened, and it wasn't going to happen.

"You need to pull yourself together, girl," Alex said aloud to herself. What the hell was even wrong with her? Was she tripping just because he was so attractive? She ought to know better! Alex had a loving husband, and even if the sex wasn't what she wanted, she wasn't going to mess shit up by screwing around with her husband's protégé. That would be a hell of an entanglement, and she wasn't interested in any of that shit. All she needed to do was get laid like never before by Amir. Alex hoped her husband would make her cum so hard that all dirty thoughts of Jay would disappear into thin air.

Downstairs, Jay and Amir sat on the patio, taking in a view of the acres of well-trimmed lawn and trees. The cool Buckhead breeze greeted Jay as he took in the view. He had always dreamed of a penthouse high up in the sky in busy Atlanta, but he was having a second thought. He kind of liked the serenity. Maybe he could have both; a place with some peace and calm like this, and another home with the city traffic stories below.

"I just want to thank you again for doing this with me," Jay said. Brenda had told him of some kid, who Amir had wanted to mentor. She had to do a lot of convincing for Jay to jump in line ahead of him, and he in turn had put in a lot of nights over at her apartment.

"We do what we can. Being Black in Hollywood is tough, even if America says it is evolving. We rise by lifting others. When I got into Hollywood years ago, I had very seasoned actors who guided me. I am talking about actors like Philip Eugene, Charles Danata, Roman Knowles," Amir rattled out his mentors.

"No way," Jay said, adding some excitement to his voice. However, he already knew Amir's back story. He knew a lot more about this man than he let on. He knew how much Amir had been paid for his first gig. He actually knew the very first apartment Amir had lived in. The only things he didn't know about Amir was his personal life which he kept private. The internet was an amazing place to find a lot about a person. It was easier with Amir being a celebrity, with his business snooped into regularly. He had also gotten personal tidbits from Brenda who spilled everything he wanted as he pounded into her pussy. She had given him all the ins into Amir's business. She had also done a thorough job convincing Amir to take him on as a protégé.

Jay had started piping Brenda about six months ago. This particular get-together was held at Bruno's house, with some movie director who loved to throw wild parties. He had bought the latest Armani fit, almost spending all his paycheck, knowing he would reap the benefits with the hookups he would make. Sure enough, there had been a lot of cougars at the party. But the one that had caught his attention had been Brenda. Hell, he had been trying to get a hold of her for a while after finding out she was Amir's agent but to no avail. Lucky for him she had liked what she saw, and had slipped him her room number, in a hotel a few rides away. That night, he had his dick buried inside of her while she screamed his name. He hadn't fucked her for real, for real. Nah, he had given her a tip of what he could do, and the following day she had his phone ringing off the hook. Jay took the dick away from her for two weeks- starved her. Then he finally caved in when she bought him a Rolex. She was a needy chick, and he knew exactly how to handle women like that.

A few months ago, he had started pressuring her to hook him up with Amir. She had been reluctant at first, then he had pulled away, taking with him his dick. Of course, she had come begging for his dick, literally dropping on the floor, with a promise that she would hook him up with Amir. And here he was, months later, in Amir's home!

"True. These men helped pave the way for me. I probably would still be struggling, you know," Amir reminisced. Or as Alex would tell him, he would have worked twice as hard to get to where he was. Whatever the way, he was grateful for how far he had come.

Chef Collins had been Alex's personal chef before they got married. His cuisine was excellent, even a burger tasted like heaven. And if you needed a salad, it tasted divine. He knew how to cook every dish on the planet, and if he didn't know, he learned. The Chef rolled in a trolley filled with their breakfast. Two maids robed with black dresses assisted him.

Jay barely watched the setup, but he was damn excited. This was like a five-star hotel! Being served by some chef. Damn! He couldn't wait to get to this level of success. Bacon. Steaks. Eggs. Pancakes. Toast. Sala. Freshly squeezed orange juice. Is that pure gold cutlery? He wondered from the corner of his eyes.

"Thank you, Collins," Amir said, spreading a napkin on his laps.

"Collins, everything is looking good this morning," Alex said, walking into the patio.

Jay perked at her voice, his dick slightly raising.

Collins smiled.

"So Jay, did you grow up in Atlanta?" Amir asked, placing some bacon on his plate.

"Yeah I did. Born and bred in Atlanta," Jay said. He never gave many people his true backstory, because then they would know he had grown up dirt poor. Not that he gave a shit, but in the movie industry, appearances were key. He had never looked poor. As a kid, even if he had to sleep on the floor at home, he showed up in school wearing new Timberlands. No one would believe he had grown up in the ghetto unless he told them. His needs had always been provided for him by the women in his life.

Women had always gravitated to Jay since he was a little boy. He had been a cute child. And as he grew older, those flirting eyes of theirs had started following him, wanting a piece of him. He had sexed his first woman at fifteen, his teacher who had rewarded him with an A. Miss Price had a body made by Mattel, and had taught him how to eat out a woman. She had indeed given him after-school lessons at her apartment where he also screwed her over countless times in any position she wanted.

After her, had been an innumerable number of women, and his love for older women grew greatly. They were experienced and had taught him how to please a woman, rewarding him in various ways. Unlike the women his age, they didn't ask for money, neither did they ask for faithfulness. As a matter of fact, they were quite generous with their money and their body. Most of all, there was no drama with them. From time to time, he tried to deal with women his age, and was only reminded of why he shouldn't deal with them. They were so freaking loud and crass, and always up in his business. And in the bed, they laid there, wanting him to do all the work. He found that older women were like fine wine. They were delicious. And they took care of him.

"You okay Mrs. Sheldon?" Jay asked, as he took a bite of a sandwich.

Alex's eyes flew to him. She had deliberately pulled away from the conversation, avoiding his gaze. She was fighting with her control, just being around him, and it was so damn difficult. His voice was sending sizzles to her coochie. She really did need to snap out of it.

"Mrs. Sheldon?" Amir laughed with a mouthful.

"Don't call me that. I hate being called that like I'm an old headmistress." Alex returned.

"But you ain't old. You are far from being old," Jay said. He meant every word he said. She was 100% natural, with that curvy body, and those firm breasts that he couldn't wait to get his hands on. She barely had on makeup and there were no wrinkles on her face. How many twenties could boast of such gorgeousness?

Alex took a long sip from her glass, taking in deep breaths.

Amir chuckled. "You got a smooth mouth there, fella. Gonna help you with your female fans, because they are wild. They're crazy as hell!"

Jay chuckled. Yeah, he did know how crazy they could be. Brenda had told him a lot of stories about Amir's crazy female fans, and how Amir never strayed.

"They haven't started hitting on you?" Amir asked.

Jay had starred in a couple of ads for weird products: a camping tent, a vacuum flask, and had worn a bear outfit. He had also played minor roles in a few TV shows. However, most of his income came from his female sponsors. He did have his share of female fans, who didn't give a shit about the movies he had starred in. All they saw was a hot body and a penis. "Nah," Jay replied.

"Don't worry, you soon will," Amir said.

"Do you have male admirers?" Jay directed at Alex.

Her glass almost fell over, but she quickly tightened her grip on it.

Amir laughed a little. He liked this kid. "She does. Lots of niggas promising her the world, sending over flowers and chocolate. You know one even got her a plane ticket to an all-expense paid vacation to Turks and Caicos, but she's my woman and we ride together," Amir declared, reaching for his wife's hand.

With a smile, Alex held on to him. Yeah, he was right. They rode together, with no room for third parties.

Jay grinned. He recognized the look in Alex's eyes. It was that of a woman who cared for her husband, but who was sexually deprived. Fortunately, he was just the right person she needed.

CHAPTER SIX

Alex sat in bed with her glasses, reading through the scriptures. She was doing more of it lately. It was her way of fighting the temptation that had come into her home in the form of Jay.

"You okay?" Amir asked, as he adjusted his tie. Alex had been somewhat withdrawn in the past week. He kept on asking her if something was wrong, but she always replied in the positive. But he could feel her pulling away.

"Yes, I am. Just got a bit of a headache," Alex answered, running her fingers through her scalp. There he went again with those pondering questions.

He sat with concern by her side. "What's wrong honey? You wanna have that checked?"

"I think I am just stressed. This management stuff got me going back to school. Always hated that shit, ya know," Alex flashed a smile.

Alex chuckled. Yeah, school had freaking sucked. Lots of bullshit was taught that would not be used in the real world.

"Don't worry babe, you gonna own this shit. I believe in you," Amir said, placing a kiss on her lips. "I'm gonna run now. Got to catch up with Jay. He has great potential, but has a whole lot of work to do. Got to polish the hell out of him."

As much as he wanted to help Jay, his skills needed plenty of development. He had a handsome face and welcoming presence, but acting was more than that. There was only so far good looks could take you. But Jay was a hustler. He wasn't out to play games. He had some steel to him that showed he was ready to work his ass off. And those were the type of people Amir enjoyed working with. He had worked with actors who were far worse than Jay, and made them better versions of themselves.

"Nobody said it was gonna be easy," Alex reminded him. She was tempted to tell him to drop Jay. But what reason would she give? Hey Amir, so your protégé is hot, and I want to fuck him? Amir would drop him if she told him about her attraction to the kid, but at the same time, his insecurities would rear their head. And she would have more than a lot on her table. Every time he saw some young dude walk past, he would ask her if she was attracted to him as well, or if there was just something different about Jay. Who wants to go through that?

"Exactly. You want me to make an appointment with Phil?" he asked, referring to their family doctor.

She waved dismissively. "I will just take an aspirin, and rest for a while before heading out."

"Okay honey. See you later."

Alex waited for the car to drive down the driveway, then counted to twenty before getting out of bed. She slipped out of her satin robe, letting it drop to the ground as she walked to the bathroom but not before reaching to the back of her closet to retrieve her sex toy. She sat on the edge of the tub running a warm bath, and sprinkled some of her bath salt. Then she got in.

Alex moaned in delight. The aromas of the salt intoxicating her, as the warmth of the water offered its embrace. She grabbed her dildo, and let the water moisten it before slipping it into her folds.

Her eyes shut close from the beautiful feeling that welcomed her. She gasped as the dildo slid into her, wishing she had a warm body to hold on to. A warm body like Jay. Her eyes flew open at the thought. She tried to bury the thought, just as she had tried in the past days, but it was too late. Alex bit on her lips imagining him shoving his dick in her. She would bet her last dollar that he was long and thick. A growl escaped her lips. She thrust the dildo in with one hand and played with her nipples with the other. She loved and hated masturbation. It gave her all the orgasms she needed, but at the same time, it was one-sided.

"Jay!" she cried as she imagined those eyes of his staring at her. All through breakfast a week ago, he had thrown innuendos at her, that had gone way over Amir's head, otherwise he would have kicked him out. As much as she tried to tell herself that she was imagining it, that kid wanted to bang her.

"Jayyyyyy!" Alex moaned sensuously as her body racked with an orgasm. Her body fell back against the bath as she took soft breaths. She continued with the rest of the bath, her body now energized for the day.

Alex was almost dressed when the phone rang. She snarled. It was Keisha calling. Now what did that heifer want?

"What do you want Keisha?" Alex snapped.

"Who that fine nigga I just seen with your husband?" Keisha asked with thirst.

"Who are you talking about?" Alex asked, confused.

"Fine looking dude. He is young as hell. Got a ponytail. Got a mouth that looks like it can do some thangs," Keisha added with that irritating laugh that Alex disliked.

"Umm... If he has a ponytail, then I think that's Jay, Amir's new protégé. Yeah that's Jay," Alex said.

"Damn! You and your husband picked a hella fine protégé. You sure that mentoring shit ain't a cover for threesomes? Tell me sister, you know you can trust me. I want in on this mentoring shit if it involves fine niggas like Jay."

"Keisha, is that why you called me? Seriously?" Alex asked with an eyeroll.

"Hell, I need to know who the hell he is. Got me dripping already, and I need to call shotgun. So you not interested in him?"

"No, I am not. I am married, Keisha!"

"So am I, and I still love dick."

"Keisha! Is there something else you need?"

Keisha laughed. "You got his number? Let me hit him up. I need that really bad."

"No, I don't have his number. But you have Amir's. Why don't you call him up, and stop disturbing me?" She hung up before Keisha could say something else stupid.

It was good that Keisha had taken an interest in Jay. This meant he was off the table; it was not as if she was interested in doing anything with him anyway. That was if Jay loved older women. He was a young looking man, and it seemed logical that he would go after young women like him, instead of a woman almost twice his age. Perhaps, Jay flirting with her had just been her imagination.

*

"Is everything okay?" Jay asked when Amir returned. He had stepped away to take a call. They were at a private country club which could only be accessed by VIP card holders and their guests. Out of curiosity, Jay had googled the access while Amir was away taking his phone call, and the numbers made his eyes widened. $200k yearly for this crappy club? With their watered-down cocktails and dry sandwiches? Folks did waste a lot of money on nonsense.

However, as he waited for Amir to return, he spotted a lot of familiar faces in the entertainment industry. He had seen one old director from the industry named Jimmy who was in his seventies, walk in with some busty chick who couldn't have been a day over nineteen. He obviously liked his women the age of his granddaughters. Jimmy was seated with Ronny, a FOX newscaster and some of his buddies who were also in entertainment. As Jay looked around, he realized this was more than some country club, it was a hangout spot for celebrities. That $200k was for networking.

"Amir!" Seun clapped Amir on the back.

Seun who was originally from Nigeria was the creator of a popular African show that had gotten him several nominations and awards. He was an acquaintance of Amir, and had been trying to persuade him to be a guest star on his show.

"Seun. How are you doing man?"

"Damn good. You holding out on me man. You know that, right?"

Amir laughed. "I will have Alex call you, she's managing me now. Perhaps we can do dinner sometime."

"That's good. Am up for all that." Seun paused briefly and continued on. "Hey dude! You good?"

Jay realized he was talked to him. "Uh, yes. Yes, I am," he replied then shook hands as Amir made the introductions.

"Welcome Jay. You should hook him up with Katrina, we need some actors for our new season," Seun said, as someone called to him. "I will see you later. Don't forget that dinner bro!"

"Katrina is his manager for Off the Boats," Amir said, referring to the TV series Seun directed. "He's really supportive towards young actors. You will never guess who I was just talking to on the phone."

Jay shook his head, taking a sip from his cocktail. Now the drink seemed to taste better, probably because he might have just gotten a role, even if it was on some crappy African show.

"Keisha. She's Alex's friend."

"Keisha?"

"Yeah, Keisha Robinson, she's married to—"

"Daniel Robinson," Jay interrupted. Yeah, he knew Keisha Robinson. She had a reputation for loving to sleep with young men and women. He had spotted her at a few parties from a distance but she never appealed to him. From what he had gathered, she was a cougar in all sense. She chewed up and spat out, draining her victims with her manipulations. And worse, she was stingy; there would be very few gifts, if any, given by her.

"She was leaving the club and saw us then called Alex and asked about you," Amir said, shaking his head in amusement.

"She did? What did Alex say?" Jay asked, curious.

"She told her you are working with me," Amir hesitated as if choosing his next words wisely. "Uh, before I continue on, here is the disclaimer. Stay away from Keisha! She's a beast, and shouldn't be played with. You don't want her around you. She's going to mess up your career." Amir took a deep breath. "Now she said I should give her your number, but I ain't doing that shit. I'm not gonna ruin your life."

Jay chuckled. Keisha was a cougar, but the next time their paths crossed, he was now determined to turn the table on her. She was experienced, but he wasn't some young naïve cat that could be fooled by a kitten. He might be twenty-five years old, but he had a lifetime of knowledge about women. However, he wasn't interested in her sex. Not yet anyway.

"I'm serious, man. She promises the world to her victims, then later discards them like trash on the street. And they don't call her out because they are scared of the repercussions. Now, I don't know the kind of women you like, but avoid women like that. You focus on women this early in your career, and you are not going to go far. Focus on the bag. And when you want to settle down, go for a woman who won't give you a bunch of problems because that's one foot closer to the grave or being broke," Amir advised.

His advice had done a lot of good to many young actors and actresses who followed through. Drugs, women/men, bling, and all that shit were all distractions, and they could easily lead one off the right track. There were some successful men who he had looked up to, who were now dead broke, and on the streets, because they had spent their money on women, booze and drugs. Their life stories always gave Amir the strength to stay focused on his path.

"Oh, I got my eyes on the bag all right. To the bag!" Jay toasted, as Alex's striking body came to mind.

"To the bag," Amir agreed.

*

Jay got into his apartment later in the day. It was a small apartment which cost $1,000 per month, but he didn't have to worry about that because he had a three year lease paid by one of the women he had been dating at the time. She had also provided the funds for furnishing it. He shrugged out of his coat and hung it on a coat hanger, then went to find some food in the fridge. They had been fed finger food at the club and he was damn hungry. He returned to the living room a few minutes later with a bowl of ramen. His phone rang at that moment. It was Brenda calling.

"Hey Jay, how has the coaching been with Amir?" Brenda asked, popping gum which she was so fond of doing.

"He's a cool dude," Jay said with a shrug.

"I told you. You met Alex?" Brenda asked.

"Yeah," Jay replied.

"Such a stuck-up bitch," Brenda cackled. When he didn't agree with her immediately, she added, "Wait, you must like her. Is she your type?"

"Nah, he's hot though. How did he land a chick like that?" Jay said.

"She's the one who's damn lucky. You look at Amir? Now, he's the one who is freaking hot. He can have any woman he wants, but he stays faithful to the old lady. She is the one who's lucky. So don't even think of trying to hit on her. Don't try that shit, Jay. Don't fucking do that. She's gonna rat your ass out to Amir, and your career gonna be gone," Brenda ranted.

Jay gave a menacing laugh.

"Am serious. That's how she is. Those folks got eyes for only each other. Don't screw up your career trying to get some pussy. Amir can make one phone call and have you black-balled. Don't be stupid. Please don't make me regret recommending you. Understand?"

"I hear you clearly, Brenda. I ain't into her," Jay lied sensing a little jealousy tied in with her concerns.

"Good. So when are you coming over?" Brenda asked.

"You dumped that dick? What's his name?" He was referring to the new dude Brenda was screwing. Some skinny ass dude whom he was pretty sure liked men too.

"That idiot can't suck a pussy like you do," Brenda whined.

He laughed, as he looked at his watch. "I will see if I can come over later."

After ending the call with Brenda, Jay relaxed on the couch. He definitely wasn't going over to Brenda's house tonight. Shit had kind of ended between them, and he didn't want her to hop back thinking she could call for his dick any time she wanted. While he might give her the occasional screw once in a while, he had set his eyes on a new target. Alex Sheldon.

Alexandria was all he could think of when lying in bed or in the shower stroking his cock. No woman had gotten into his head like Alex had. There were so many things he wanted to do to her. Soooo many things! She seemed tough and untouchable. But he knew a lot about women. He knew she wanted him. He had read it in her eyes. Her husband wasn't making it happen in the bed. He might buy diamonds for her, but he wasn't a pussy or bedroom connoisseur as Jay knew himself to be. He was determined to light up her world, she would think of no one else but him.

CHAPTER SEVEN

What the hell was he doing here? Alex stared at the intercom screen, watching Jay as he stood out there at the gates. Amir was out of town, and would not be back until tomorrow, so what was he doing there?

"I know you can see, Alex," Jay joked.

"Amir is not home, Jay," Alex said, after a moment.

Jay's voice became serious, "You know I came to see you. Let me in."

"What are you talking about?" Alex's anxiety heightened. She took a deep breath. She never thought it would happen like this. Her fantasies had played out completely different. Then she thought of every reason why letting him in would be the worst decision of her life. Hell no! Just as she was about to tell him to get the hell away from her gate, she pressed the buzzer and the gates opened, letting him in.

Alex stood in the picture window watching Jay walk across the lawn wearing a cocky smile on his face. She rolled her eyes thinking she should have left his ass out there, but she had a feeling he wouldn't have left, and his presence could attract attention.

Jay's Uber had dropped him off at the gate so he was willing to wait forever for Alex to let him in. He knew Amir was away, and would be back tomorrow. He also knew she was home alone. He had slipped in an innocent question about the live-in staff, and Amir had told him by afternoon they were out of the house every day, unless there were prior instructions. So, Jay had timed it perfectly. It was just him and Alex alone. His dick hardened. He had been waiting for this day for weeks now, and it was pure torture. Every time he came over, they had no idea the kind of control it took for him not to mount her right in front of her husband.

The door opened with his hand hanging for a knock. Damn she looked scrumptious! Alex had on a T-shirt which molded her breasts with high-waisted jeans. Her face was bare of makeup, and he stared at her lips, imagining them wrapped around him.

"What do you want?" Alex snapped, her skin on fire from the heat of his gaze. She should never have let him in, she realized too late.

"You gonna let me stand out here?" Jay asked.

Alex stepped aside, letting him in, then shutting the door close. She turned around and gasped, he was in her space. "Jay, I don't know what you—"

"You know what I want. You know it," Jay whispered, leaning forward to take a deep breath of that fragrance that was tantalizing his senses, Bond No. 9 Madison Square Park.

She tried pushing him away but he didn't budge. "Move away, Jay. Letting you come in here was a mistake. I need you to—"

Jay kissed her, tasting those lips he had wanted from the first day he came to her home. Still in surprise, and as expected, she pushed him away. His arms wrapped around her, pulling her back to him.

"Let go!" Alex struggled against him.

He had never forced a woman, unless she wanted him to. And if that was Alex's desires, he was ready to give in, but not now. What this woman needed was some good loving. He grabbed her hand and placed it on his hardened rod. Alex's eyes widened. She tried to pull away as he began to caress his hard-on with her hands.

"I want to taste you then fuck you, Alex. We both know you want that. We both know you think of me when you fuck yourself with your dildo."

"How—"

Jay chuckled. "How do I know? Because I excel in knowing women and a woman like you who needs to be fucked often, definitely has a dildo. Why use that shit when you got the real deal here? I won't tell, unless you tell."

Alex shook her head in refusal, but her hand on its own accord kept stroking his shaft. She could feel it pulsing. It was exactly how she had imagined it. Long and thick. She yelped as he lifted her, his hands on her ass, as her legs wrapped around his waist. Her back met the wall as his lips descended on hers. This time around, she didn't protest. She moaned as he nibbled on her lips, his hands descending on her boobs, kneading them softly. Then he pulled some type of magic that caused her pants and panties to disappear.

"Jay, we—" His tongue slid into her as his hands went under her blouse.

"You taste good," Jay groaned as he kissed her below, his fingers tracing the lace bra she had on. Her breasts were full and firm as he suspected. He pulled away from her and before she could protest, he had her blouse over her head, tossing it to the ground. He stared in awe at those luscious tits in front of him.

Alex felt the need to cover her breasts. No man had looked at her in such a way. In hunger. "Jay we should—"

He stopped her by placing his finger on her lips. "Ssssh." Then he groaned as her tongue flicked out on its own accord, sucking his finger in.

"You are such a bad girl Alex, aren't you?" Jay hissed as she sucked harder on his finger. She nodded. Her eyes rolled to the back as his other hand enveloped her boobs, pushing them together. She gasped in excitement releasing his finger as he swiftly removed her bra, dropping it to the ground. Then that hot mouth of his blew on her nipple, as he sucked hard on it.

"Jayyyyyyy!" Alex cried, holding on to him as he sucked harder, his other hand kneading her other breast softly.

He wanted more of her, to taste every inch of her body. He wanted her legs spread on the bed and suck the heart of her femininity. But he couldn't wait. He lifted her and placed her on the couch. She was a beautiful sight before him, her legs still wrapped around him, her nipples still erect, with her hair a tumbled mess.

They drew closer at the same time, their lips smashing as he teased her boobs, massaging them, earning moans from her.

"I need to feel you," Alex cried.

He let go of her for an instance, lifting his shirt up, and dumping it on the ground. Alex stared at his chest hungrily. He was hard everywhere. Her eyes drifted down, going to his trouser which hung low on his waist. He grabbed her, her breasts smashing against his chest as his fingers entangled in her hair. Alex gyrated against him, moaning. Her juices seemed to be pouring out of her! She was wetter than she had ever been.

"You're so sexy," Jay mumbled as his tongue planted kisses down her neck. He pulled at her nipple with his fingers, his mouth sucking hard on the other one. She mumbled, wanting more as he pulled away from her, sliding down her stomach.

Alex froze as he hovered above her admiring her freshly shaven mound. This caused her essence to release a flood. She was sure he could see the wet spot she had caused. Jay was now moving in an intoxicating pace that almost frustrated her. She smiled as he groaned, looking at her with hunger then slowly parting her outer lips. First, he flicked her clit with his tongue as if playing with it, before she could say anything, he started tongue kissing her pearl slowly yet with such precision. Then without warning he darted his tongue into her core tasting the sweetness of her juices.

Alex thought she died, went to heaven, and came back. That was the only way she could describe what she was feeling. That tongue of his was divine. It was so long, dipping into her folds, as his fingers also took their turn. Her legs clenched around his neck, as her fingers tugged at his hair.

"Jaaaaaayyyyy!" she cried loudly as he ate her with such hunger it felt like his last meal.

Jay loved pussy. But Alex's had him on another level. The musky smell, her clean taste, and even her love box's gorgeous brown folds. He wanted to give his devotion to it all night long. Her moans made him eat her with more intensity. He loved those sounds as they caused his member to pulsate, making him harder. He stared up for a moment, taking into his memory the look of pleasure on her face as his fingers danced in her hot lava. This was how a woman should look when she was being pleased, he reasoned.

"Fuccckkkk, I am cummmin. I'm cummmin," Alex wailed, as his tongue circled her clit. She couldn't take it anymore, her core exploded, raining all over her lover's face. Jay didn't let go of her, he gulped all of it down like a hungry child. As if that still wasn't enough, he swiped his hand down his face then licked her essence off of it, wanting to take in every drop.

Alexandria lay on the couch in a dazed state, still in shock about what had just happened. That was the most powerful orgasm she had ever had in her life. She snapped out of her state as Jay unzipped himself. Her mouth widened into an O, as his staff sprung out. Her love box riled up in renewed hunger.

"I want to suck it," Alex said, wrapping her fingers around his dick. He growled at her words.

"You will, but first I need to fuck that pussy of yours. You have no idea how much I've been wanting to do this," Jay said.

"Condom!" Alex demanded, coming slightly to her senses.

Jay grabbed a packet from his pocket. Alex grinned, and he smirked. Yeah, he had come prepared, confident of how it would end. She took the packet from him, and tore it open. He groaned as those hands of hers tortured his dick, rolling the condom down on it slowly. When she was done, he grabbed her arms and placed them over her head with one hand. He held his shaft, allowing it to hover above her honeypot.

"Pleaseeee," Alex pleaded, her body lifting up to meet him as he pulled away. The heat from his cock was frustrating her. She wanted all 10 inches of him inside of her.

"How do you want it?" Jay asked.

"Hard," Alex said. A scream escaped her as he thrusted it into her. She secured her legs around his ass as he began to pound into her, harder and harder. He grabbed her boobs, playing with her nipples as he fucked her with that huge dick of his. She had never been as filled as this in her life. And she loved it.

"Look at us Alex," Jay rumbled, still driving his pole into her. "Look at how good this feels." Her lovin' felt like a luxury. Every bit of it. It was so freakin tight, taking all of him in.

"Harder!" Alex cried.

"Your pussy is so damn tight. Oh, you feel so good," Jay groaned, thrusting even harder.

"Yes, yes, yes," her moans filled the room as she had the most explosive orgasm in what seemed to be forever. She couldn't believe it topped the previous one. He kept on stroking her like his life depended on it. His stamina was the best she had ever seen in a man. Alex orgasmed two more times, before his dick stiffened in her and erupted. He collapsed onto the couch beside her, holding her in his arms.

In five years, Alex had kept her marriage vows and remained faithful to her husband. Until now. And it was the best sex of her life with incredible chemistry. What a recipe for disaster. She was not going to be able to walk properly for the rest of the day.

"I'm going to go clean up," Jay said, releasing her from his grasp. He walked naked, her eyes on his firm ass, into the foyer where there was a restroom that he had used the last time he was here. He stared in the mirror as he washed his hands. There had been no disappointments with Alex. Sex with her had been even more than he had dreamed of. Now that he'd had a taste, he wanted more. So much more.

Alex was dressed when Jay returned, wearing a frown as he had expected. Guilt, that was what she felt, but he felt none of that shit.

"This can't happen again," Alex said, becoming fully aware of what had just happened.

"Was it that bad?" Jay smirked. The sex had been great, and he knew this. Who was she kidding? It had been amazing, but this couldn't happen again. Yeah, right.

"It was a mistake. I'm married, and you're my husband's mentee. If I had a son, you would be his age! You are too young for me. You should be with a woman your age and—" She took a step back, but he pulled her to him, his hands on her ass.

"I don't like girls my age. I love women who have aged like wine," Jay whispered in her ear, earning a moan. He was sure if he tried to spread her legs at that moment, she would be more than ready.

"Oh," Alex swallowed. Why wasn't she surprised? And why was she excited as well?

"Yeah, and this is far from over, Alex. You need what I gave you and more." He silenced her with a kiss that had her moaning, as he rubbed her ass, making her cling to him. Oh yeah, he couldn't wait to get in that ass, to have his tongue buried in her ass, right before his dick went in. "Yeah you need me, your husband ain't giving it to you right. He couldn't do what I just did even if you gave him instructions. I bet he never sees the wild side of you, huh?"

Alex shook her head in denial but they both knew the truth. She acted like a good girl, but she was a bad girl in need of being set free.

"We can't do this again," Alex said weakly, as his fingers moved from her ass, stroking her now dripping pussy through her jeans.

"If you say so," Jay said with a grin.

"I mean it, Jay," Alex huffed. She frowned as he grabbed her phone. "What do you think you are doing?"

He hunched his shoulder. "Putting my number in."

"I meant what I said. This can't happen again," Alex repeated, paying attention to how his T-shirt fitted across his chest, then instantly missing the feel of that body against her.

"See you later, Alex," Jay winked as he headed for the door, pulling his Uber app up on his phone.

Alex collapsed on the couch. She wanted to believe it was all a dream, but her body was alive, evidence of the sex she had with Jay. He was twenty-five! Almost half her age. Yet why had it felt so good? He was so young, too young to make her feel better than any man ever had. She moaned as she remembered him lunching on her causing her to shower his entire face then filling her up with his length.

"Oh my goodness! What have I done?" Alex knew she was in big trouble. She had never cheated on Amir. Now she felt guilty, but at the same time there were no regrets. For so long she had lived with her desires inhibited, knowing that Jay believed in simplicity in the bedroom. And she was willing to settle for that, she reasoned. The sane thing to do was to tell Amir, but it would kill him. She shook her head at that stupid thought. Alex had no idea what was going to happen, but knew there could not be a repeat, no matter how good the sex had been.

CHAPTER EIGHT

Amir peered at his wife. There was something about Alex. However, he couldn't figure out what it was. Since he returned there had just been something odd about her.

"Why are you staring at me?" Alex asked as she added a gloss to her lips.

"Is there something you want to share with me?" Amir asked.

Alex froze. Did he know? "Um… like what?"

"Some good news. You have been quite… I dunno. You're kind of glowing. Excited. I dunno. You tell me," Amir said.

Her shoulders relaxed with relief. For a moment there, she thought he had figured out what had happened between her and Jay. It was the second day since she had sex with Jay and her body still tingled from his touch. She had tried masturbating in the aftermath, but just couldn't get herself to orgasm the way she wanted. It seemed Jay had ruined her.

"I had a massage at Spa Central two days ago, and it relieved so much stress. Maybe that's it," Alex lied.

"You having fun while I am out hustling, huh?" Amir teased, planting a kiss on her shoulder.

There was a knock on the door. It was Chef Collins. Alex went with him to a make last minute confirmation for the dinner. They were having an intimate dinner at the house with a few friends over, including Jay who Amir wanted to introduce to them. Alex had mixed feelings about this. She wanted Jay far away from their lives, but at the same time she wanted him around. She hated to admit it but she wanted to experience Jay one more time to see if it all was a fluke. Who was she kidding? Her mind, body, and spirit had not been the same since their encounter.

Chef Collins was talking to Alex but she couldn't make out a word he was saying, her mind in another world of its own with thoughts of her time with Jay. The next thing she knew she was almost dropping a plate of salad that she didn't even recall picking up. Chef steadied the plate and removed it from her hands, just in time. She flashed him an apologetic smile. "All is set for dinner. Thank you."

*

The guests started coming in at seven. The first to arrive were the Rollins, old friends of Amir, who had also become friends of Alex. They had been married for eight years with kids Alex found adorable. They brought a bottle of wine.

"You shouldn't have," Alex said, taking the bottle of wine from Trisha.

"Oh we have to. We would never show up here empty handed," Trisha laughed.

Next to arrive were the Johnsons. Alex was cool with Bridget, Matt's third wife. She was so naïve, and had no idea what was in store for her, with her asshole of a husband. He was a drunk, and was misogynistic, and had also physically abused his previous wives. The only reason Amir was friends with him was because of their business dealing,

Matt owned or had shares in several production companies, and they had established a business relationship for years.

The living room was soon occupied by several guests all chatting excitedly, as their wineglasses were refilled by the waiter, hired for the night. Alex kept looking at the door, in anticipation for Jay's arrival. She hadn't seen him since that day, and hoped her topnotch acting skills would make her behave like things were normal, as they were.

"Who's that fine stud," Janet said.

Alex's eyes followed Janet's and rested on Jay who had just arrived, and was receiving quite the admiring glances, especially from the women. He had on a black leather jacket, that screamed bad boy.

In her forties, Janet was a director's nightmare. Demanding, rude, abusive, and selfish, she was difficult to work with despite her pretty face. She had gotten away with it, in her younger years, but with the industry now more open to black actors, Janet had been passed over by many directors. This made her acting career go on somewhat of a hiatus, except for roles given to her either out of pity or persuasion from some of Janet friends. She wasn't fun to be around either, especially with her flirtatious ways for every man in the vicinity, but she was an old friend, and Alex had decided at the last minute to fit her onto the guest list. Now Alex regretted that decision. She had forgotten how Janet had a great fondness for young men, just as many older women in the industry.

"That's Jay, Amir's mentee," Alex said, taking a long sip from her wine glass.

"I could mentor that ass all day," Janet smiled.

"He's half your age!"

Janet shrugged. "So? I mean guys his age love us. Mommy syndrome or whatever they call it. I bet he doesn't go down on girls his age. They are not the cleanest. And I also bet he fucks really good."

Thank goodness Chef Collins signaled to her, causing her to excuse herself. At that moment, she almost felt like doing something crazy like tell Janet she was damn right. Jay did screw really good. Alex hurried off, away from Jay's gaze which was now settled on her. Yes, she was running, like a child who had done something bad and didn't want to face the consequences.

However, she couldn't run for too long. As she looked over the hors d'oeuvres to approve their presentation before the waiters took them out, Jay found her in the kitchen, followed by Amir, who had an arm around his shoulder, with laughter in his eyes.

"Alex, he brought you flowers," Amir laughed.

"For the hostess. I thought of bringing wine, but I figured you have tons of that already," Jay said.

"Umm… thank you Jay. This was… thoughtful of you," Amy said, taking the flowers from him. They were red roses. For passion, she read in his eyes, quickly looking away.

"Let's go settle down for dinner. Got a lot of people I want you to meet tonight," Amir said, as he headed out.

Jay didn't want to leave. He wanted to tell Alex that she was the most beautiful woman here tonight in that sexy red dress with thin straps. He wanted to tell her that he had missed her. He hoped he hadn't made a mistake by giving her some time to herself, and not bombarding her with texts and calls. He knew what he had between his legs was addictive but by the look on Alex's face, he now wasn't so sure about that.

"Jay! You coming?" Amir called from the hallway when he realized he was alone.

"Sure, Amir!" Jay bellowed. He threw Alex a look then turned on his heels leaving her alone.

There were even more guests when Amir and Jay returned to the living room, and Jay recognized two of them. The first was Robert Grey, he had started out as a musician in the eighties, and Jay had grown up listening to his sister dancing to his songs. A short role in a TV series had made Robert realize he had acting potential, that's when he made a switch that had created an even more successful career. His wife, Naomi was a renowned celebrity who was always on suing someone for something. Now their daughter, Summer, he already knew from afar. She was a model who hung with a group of spoiled rich kids like her. They spent all day shopping, on Instagram and travelling, as well as clubbing. She was hot, with her boobs spilling out of her gown in a tacky way. She was twenty-five. It was pretty obvious she had gone under the knife a couple of times. He could feel her eyes on him, trying to get his attention. Too bad, he wasn't interested. All she would bring to his life was drama.

"Amir! You don't age a bit! Where's your gorgeous wife? I didn't come here for you, you know?" Robert teased as they gave bro hugs.

Amir chuckled. "I know, asshole. She's in the kitchen rounding up things. Naomi, are you tired of your husband yet?" Amir asked as he hugged her.

Naomi laughed. "You will be the first person to know when I am."

"This is my new protégé. Name's Jay," Amir introduced.

Parties were a great way to introduce a newbie to experienced people in the industry. They created a calm and interactive atmosphere and someone always benefitted when there were key figures in attendance.

"Nice to see you, Jay. Been in any movie I have seen?" Robert asked.

"Griffin," Jay said. That was the most successful of his movie, and that was an overstatement. Griffin had been a flop and the only reason it had gained attention was because a scene from it had been used as a meme.

"Oh, probably why you look familiar," Robert said.

Jay could see through that shit. No way Robert had watched that shitty movie. He had a horrible filmography filled with movies made by low budget producers and cast. He had realized he couldn't keep wasting his talent on such bullshit, and had to step it up. In a year's time, there would be no need for introductions. People would recognize him just by his face.

"You were that dude who died right at the beginning?" Summer asked, slipping a hand into his.

"Yes," Jay said, not surprised she had seen the movie. It was more common with millennials.

"Smile for the camera," Summer said, as she took a selfie of them. "Hashtag, I just met— What's your name?" she looked up as she typed on her phone.

"Jay Carlo," Jay said. He was going to have a lot of followers from this single post. Damn networking was lit!

"You're gonna be my plus one. Hope this party won't be such a bore because it is full of oldies. I don't know why my parents made me come," Summer said, pulling him along.

He had wanted to sit close to Alex, where he could talk to her all through the night, but knew that probably wasn't a good idea.

A woman stopped them on the way to the table, pushing her breasts in his face. His nose scrunched at her heavy perfume. "Jay darling. We should talk sometime later. You and I," she added with a wink, slipping her card into his pocket, before walking away seductively.

"You should get rid of that card. She carries every disease there is in the world. Herpes, Gonorrhea, everything," Summer advised.

Jay nodded. He had no intention of screwing her anyway. He avoided women like that. They were desperate and wanted to drain his youth then kick him out the door. He went for more refined women, just like the woman who had just walked in. Alex glanced at him briefly, then said hello to the guests who had just come in.

Dinner started out great. Conversation revolved around gossip, new releases, collaborations; basically, just news circulating around the movie industry. Jay kept on a straight face listening to all of the conversations. He was shocked that there was so much going on right under his nose he wouldn't even know unless he was in the inner caucus, where information circulated freely.

"Jay, do you have a girlfriend?" Janet asked.

Conversation hushed instantly, everyone anticipating his reply, especially Janet's response to it. She had not hidden the fact from the onset of dinner that she wanted Jay.

"Yes, I do," Jay replied.

Janet smiled. "That makes it even better."

Summer playfully gagged beside Jay as he stifled his laughter with a sip of his wine. He turned to Alex who was toying with her wine glass.

Alex retreated to her thoughts. So, Jay had a girlfriend? She shouldn't be surprised. He was a young, sexy man, with women, both young and old throwing themselves at him. Which meant she was just another notch on his bed. She berated herself quickly, for even thinking there might be something for her there. It had just been a one-time thing. Never to repeat itself again.

"You okay? You haven't eaten much," Amir observed quietly.

"Something is off with my appetite today, babe." Alex said, flashing a smile.

"I hope you have enough appetite for me tonight," Amir leaned forward to whisper. Alex laughed, earning a look from Jay who frowned. It irritated him to see them so close to each other. The envy was clear on his face although he knew Amir couldn't begin to satisfy Alex.

"Umm... you okay?" Summer asked.

Jay realized he was clenching his spoon. He flashed his gorgeous smile at his companion. "Of course."

An hour later, dinner was done, with the guests spread in the living room and patio. Alex went upstairs. She could feel a headache kicking in and needed to pop in some aspirins. She stepped out of her shoes, walking barefooted to the bathroom. The room door opened and she yelled to Amir, "Honey! I am in here! Got this crazy headache!"

She was received with silence. "Amir?" Alex gasped at the person who walked into the bathroom. "What the hell are you doing in here?"

"Your room is beautiful. Warm tones and—"

"I don't give a shit about what you think of my room, Jay! What are you doing here? Are you crazy? You can't just walk into my room! My husband is downstairs! With guests! You need to leave now!" She grabbed his arm, heading for the door. She couldn't believe he had the audacity to come into her room. Was he crazy?

Jay pulled her back, pressing her body to his. "Chill. No one saw me come in. Besides I locked the door," he grinned.

She glared in return. What nerve! "I don't give a shit, get out Jay! That shit that happened, forget about it. Understand?" She tried to free herself from him, but Jay was having none of it. "Let me go you idiot!" she snapped.

In response, his lips lowered to hers. She groaned as her lips betrayed her, by parting, letting him in. She shook her head. Hell no! They weren't going to do this with her husband and guests downstairs.

"You think too much, Alex," Jay said as he grabbed her breast through her dress.

Alex squealed at the pain which excited her. She motioned her head in refusal, as he slid the straps of her dress down. His eyes widened as he stared at her firm boobs once again.

Alex moaned as he toyed with her hard nipples, squeezing them gently, as his tongue flicked around them. She was boiling hot already! Honestly, she had been horny from the moment he walked in.

There was no resistance as he placed her on the bed. He lifted her gown, and before she could say anything, he thrust into her. She gasped as she felt his sheathed dick in her. The asshole had worn a condom already! She glared at him, and he grinned at her, as his dick thrust harder into her.

Alex wanted to scream. She wanted to yell at him to do her as he had done before, but there were guests downstairs! Forget the guests, her husband was downstairs while Jay was upstairs stroking as if his life depended on it.

"Jayyyy pleaseee," she begged in a whisper.

"What do you want?" Jay growled.

"Harrddderrr," Alex cried.

He obliged, going harder into her, as her fingers dug into the sheets.

"Yess! Yess!" she cried as he pinched her nipples. She had never had a man take her this way. Not like a doll, but as a woman, capable of being fucked. Her body crumbled as the piercing orgasm overwhelmed her. She couldn't take it anymore. She came, her body giving in as Jay continued to fuck her.

He flipped her over and stroked her from the back, doggy-style, pounding in even harder and deeper. She could feel another orgasm building up.

"I'm about to let it go baby. Squeeze that cum out of me!" Jay groaned as they orgasm together. Pleasured, he managed to let go of her and fell on the bed, next to her.

Alex's eyes closed sleepily. In just a few days, she had been screwed like never before, and she still wanted more. She remained insatiable. She could go all night but... she jolted out of the bed.

"You need to get out of here!" Alex said, shaking him.

"Why?" Jay sighed.

She gave him an implausible look, wondering if he was indeed crazy. If she was gone for too long, Amir was going to come find her.

"Fine, but I want to see you tomorrow." Jay grumbled as he zipped his trousers up. I mean it," he added when she shook her head 'no'. Still drawn to her, he grabbed Alex and planted a kiss on her lips before leaving the room.

Alex hurried to the bathroom. Her makeup was still intact but she touched it up anyway. Just as she applied a new coat of gloss on her lips, the room door opened. She scowled thinking Jay was back. Just as she was about to yell at him, Amir showed up at the doorway, with a plate of dessert.

"It is almost finished. But I saved some for you," Amir said, handing the plate to her.

"Oh... Thank you," Alex said, taking the plate from him.

"You okay?" Amir asked.

"Sure. I just needed to fix up a bit. Let's go downstairs before our guests think we abandoned them," Alex said, taking her husband's hand.

"Time for a quickie?" Amir chuckled.

There was no laughter on Alex's face. It would definitely be a quickie. "Uh, not now dear. I have a headache. Probably stress from planning the party."

Their guests hadn't missed them when they returned. Everyone was partnered up in a discussion. Summer was all over Jay, telling him about her friends, while Janet was literally screwing Jay from the end of the room where she was having a conversation. If they were alone, she shuddered to think what the woman would do to Jay.

The party ended a few hours later, with the Sheldons seeing their guests off to the front door. Jay was going to be dropped off by the Jones who were heading his way.

"I enjoyed myself, Amir. Alex. A lot," Jay added, his gaze lingering on Alex, who glared at him, at the innuendo.

"I am glad you did. My home is always open to you," Amir said.

There was laughter in Jay's eyes that Alex wanted to wipe off. He was finding all of this humorous, but she found it exasperating. She'd had sex with him on her matrimonial bed. It was just crazy! She should know better than even associate with Jay, but despite having two tastes of him, she wanted more. With that gaze in his eyes, he promised her of more pleasure to come. What she was doing was wrong, and it was smart to put an end to it now, but she just couldn't stop. At least not yet.

As Alex settled into bed that night, her phone buzzed with a message. Her eyes widened as she stared at the screen.

Jay: I wish you were here with me so I can spread your pussy wide and feast on you till morning.

How had he even gotten her number? Then she recalled him dialing his number on her phone the day they had their first session. She quickly deleted his message, but it was clear in her head. She closed her eyes, but the image remained. She rubbed her thighs together as her breath labored. She was in big trouble, and as much as it was a crazy situation, she kind of loved it.

CHAPTER NINE

Alex opened the back door and Jay walked in, holding a bag. She had given him the keys to the back gate where he could come in without drawing attention. As much as everyone minded their business, she wouldn't be surprised if some paparazzi took pictures of Jay coming in, when Amir wasn't around.

He pulled her to him, her back against the door kissing her intensely. Her body reacted to his touch. She pulled away, gasping for breath. "I need to get some wine," Alex said, walking confidently in her pink silk teddy into the kitchen. There was already a bottle of wine in the chiller on the granite island, and she grabbed some wine glasses.

"Hey," she protested as Jay pushed her against the furniture.

Alex gasped as he grabbed her breasts from behind, squeezing them roughly. He made her hurt, but she loved that pain. She hissed as he bit gently on her ear, his tongue sliding into it. He knew how much she liked that. How much that made her wet. Alex moaned louder as his tongue began to slid in and out of her ear. She imagined that tongue making love to her clit, which he was going to definitely do before he left.

"Jayyy," she started to say, as he slipped her teddy up, revealing her naked ass. She grabbed the edges of the table as his fingers found her, sliding into her bare dripping pussy.

"Always ready for me," Jay groaned in delight, rocking against her bare butt.

"Yessss," Alex cried, grinding against him as his fingers stimulated her clit then entered her. Not one, not two, but three of them. She was so full but her flower widened wanting more of him. She didn't have to say the word, he obliged, thrusting another finger into her greedy cunt. Her eyes rolled to the back as her screams filled the kitchen where she usually had breakfast with her husband. The sound of something tearing didn't register to her, until she felt his cock slip into her from behind. Her nails dug sharp into the kitchen table as he mounted her, pulling at her hair.

"You're so damn gooooddd. Your pussy is gooooldddd!" Jay swore. It never ceased to amaze him how drunk he was with her pussy. He could devour her all day, and he could fuck this pussy over and over without getting tired. It was like ambrosia, and he was addicted. Every inch of her body. Her lips. Her neck. Her feet. Her ankles. He could fuck and taste all of it, all day. "Open up for me!" he groaned as he pounded harder into her, teasing and kneading her succulent breasts.

Alex cried, literally cried as ecstasy overtook her. Her body rested for a moment, but came alive again when Jay's fingers began to play with her ass. Her body tensed for a moment then a sudden desire to be filled up by him back there came over her, but not just yet.

Minutes later, they lay on her bed intertwined, halfway through a bottle of wine. They had been screwing around for over a month now, and it was the most fun she'd had. The sex was amazing! Actually, amazing was an understatement. It was unbelievable! While sex with Amir was safe and nice, sex with Jay was wild and unexpected. She was never sure of what was going to happen. He was fire, lighting her up. The craziness was needed in her boring marriage and life filled with endless meetings and projects. She was a good girl, but with Jay, she could come alive without being scared of being judged or labelled.

"What are you thinking about?" Jay asked, pulling her naked body to him. Lying here, covered by the satin sheets, he felt fulfilled. He loved that look on her face. A well-fucked look every woman should have. He could get used to this, sexing her and having her next to him, while they drank bottle of wines.

"How great this is," Alex said. Her sexual life had been so repressed by her husband that everything Jay did seemed amazing. Amir was such a prude.

Jay grinned. Indeed, it was great. If he had a wife like Alex, he would make love to her every single night, and she would never be horny. He would do it to her all over the house, even outside for the paparazzi to see. He began to grow hard at the thought of sexing her in front of cameras. His Alex, all naked, her brown skin glistening with legs wide open. It would be quite a spread on the tabloids.

Alex giggled as his cock prodded her. With Jay, he was never tired. "You got something for me," Alex said, wrapping her fingers around his manhood. She moved down the sheets and lowered her head to it as he watched with anticipation.

Jay died a thousand deaths when those hot lips wrapped around his cock. He'd had countless women suck his cock, but Alex was the best. She was the best at everything! Her tongue slid out, licking the cum that was already dripping out. He groaned as she took him deeper, the heat of her mouth driving him nuts. Now he wanted to taste that pussy of hers.

Alex grumbled as he grabbed her ass, flipping her in one swift move onto his body. She moaned as her pussy rested on his face, his tongue sliding out to take a taste of her. A squeal escaped her lips as he slapped her ass. "Get back to work!"

This she did, turning over into the sixty-nine position, she lowered her mouth back on his cock, as his fingers slid into her pussy, with that slithering tongue of his driving her shaking body nuts.

*

Three hours later, Jay had returned to his apartment. Dread fell on him as he stripped out of his clothes. He missed Alex already. He missed the huge California king bed and those expensive sheets. He missed the beautiful spacious the house. Here, he felt caged and crappy. He wished he could spend the night with her. That he could have dinner out on the patio, and sleep next to her, then get to wake up to her beautiful face, but Amir would be home tonight. He would have to wait for some other night to be with her. As much as he loved being with

Alex, he hated the aftermath, returning home. It was a reminder of the truth; that she wasn't completely his.

He hit the shower and as the water ran over his body, he thought of Amir running his fingers through his woman's hair. Closing his eyes, he thought of Amir's head buried in his woman's pussy. He thought of Alex's face as she came, her eyes closed. In rage, he smashed his fist against the wall. He growled at the pain, his eyes flinging open.

Amir stepped out of the shower and went to the kitchen. He grabbed an almost empty bottle of whiskey and sat in front of the TV, switching through the stations. He finally stopped at a medical drama, which he was fond of. Usually, he would watch with interest, picking up the mannerisms of the characters, but not today. All he could think about was Alex.

He grabbed his phone and dialed her number. It rang. Twice, but she didn't answer. Now he was worried. What was she doing? Was she fucking Amir who could not satisfy her? He had no idea why she hadn't kicked him out of her life a long time ago. She was a beautiful and desirable woman who could have any man she wanted. A woman who could have him. She didn't need Amir. Outside of money, he had nothing to offer her. Now, the fourth ring.

"Jay?"

He snapped out of his thoughts as he realized he had called Amir. "Umm… hey Amir!" Jay replied.

"It's late, Jay. Is everything okay?" Amir asked with concern.

Alex, who was taking care of her nighttime skin routine, stopped in front of the mirror at the mention of her lover's name.

"Uh yeah. I just wanted to say… Uh thanks for everything you do. You know the gig with Seun," Jay said with clenched fists. This role in the African drama was going to be his first lead role, and he was going to be a recurring character in a couple of episodes. He was excited about it, even though he would rather star in medical dramas, but Amir wanted him to diversify first, instead of being stereotyped.

Amir chuckled. He guessed Jay had been having a sort of realization moment, that indeed he was going to achieve his dreams that had seemed impossible. He had also had such experiences. He recalled calling Joey, one of his mentors, at midnight and interrupted the man having sex with his wife. Joey had yelled at him, asking him what he wanted. "Thank you," Amir had said. This had softened Joey only for a second, before he hung up.

"It is no bother. We're gonna do this shit together, remember?" Amir said appreciately.

"Is that Jay?" Alex asked, climbing into bed.

Jay relaxed at her voice. Only for an instance. Just imagining them together, made him wish she was with him instead.

"I'll see you Jay. Be cool," Amir said, ending the call.

Jay took a deep breath, resisting the urge to fling the phone against the wall, because he knew that was gonna cost him. His finances were a bit tight in the past months.

And this was because he cut off all of the women he was screwing for benefits. He knew Alex would get him whatever he wanted, all he needed to do was ask. But he couldn't ask her. It just didn't feel right. This was different for him. It was supposed to be the other way round. He was to care and provide for her. Not expect money and gifts from her.

Jay kind of missed the financial independence he got from messing around with those women, but ever since Alex came into his life, things had changed. Hot women, old and young flung themselves at him, but he just wasn't attracted to them. Hell, he had left Brenda in heat when he had gone over for a booty call a few days ago. As she stroked his semi-hard cock, all he could think of was Alex. No other woman amounted to her. He had heard about shit like this. Love they called it, but he had never thought it would happen to him.

Damn! But it had. Alex had ruined him for other women. The other day, his dick had refused to rise when Patricia, one of his old-timers, had come into town and they had gone on a date. It was as if he felt some sense of duty to be faithful to Alex. To be true to her, and ditch all the women in his life. And he didn't mind it. There were other ways to get money and shit from these women. He didn't have to sex them. There had been women he wouldn't screw even if he was blind, crazy women, and he had always played the game with them, knowing the right words to say. With these women he walked away with either cash or credit. Sometimes, both. So he wasn't new to being faithful.

However, he wished it was the same on Alex's part. He wished she wouldn't mess around with any other man aside from him. He wanted to be the only man who she was intimate with. The only man who got to hold her. This was a serious entanglement, he glared, taking a swig from the bottle.

CHAPTER TEN

"Damn girl! You look fineeee!" Keisha said, as Alex walked in, wearing a red pinstripe suit. She had just left a meeting with a few of Amir's agents. She had wanted to head straight home, but it had been a while since she last saw her girlfriends.

"Thank you for the compliment," Alex said. That was a rarity from Keisha.

"Someone's hitting the right spots, huh? You know you never told us how big Amir dick is," Keisha continued. The waitress who was serving them at the moment blushed, before hurrying away, as Keisha hooted.

"How have you been Alex, you have been kind of like a stranger these past months," Rita said.

"Oh, she's too good for us. Now, you some boss lady and all that shit," Keisha chided.

Ignoring her, Alex said, "I'm sorry love. Work has just been so crazy." She was taking a major step away from acting, and was spending more time on business.

"I ain't heard from that brotha. You sure Amir gave him my digits?" Keisha asked, taking a long sip from her glass.

It took Alex a second to realize the brotha she was referring to. "Oh, Jay? He has a girlfriend," Alex said.

Keisha scoffed. "Don't fucking matter. He can bring the bitch over, and I will fuck that pussy too." This time, the waitress who was right at the table scurried away.

Kim looked with irritation at Keisha.

"What?" Keisha shrugged, bugging her eyes. "He is just too fine a piece of ass for one woman to share. I bet he can "put it down" for real. Like he probably got a big dick that hits all the corners," Keisha continued dreamily, writhing on her chair.

Irritation built in Alex, but she continued to wear a plain face. However, she wanted to slap Keisha for sexualizing Jay, and at the same time tell her she was right. That dick did hit all the corners.

"You okay? I know Keisha's foul mouth works your nerves." Kim, who was next to her asked.

"Sure, I'm okay," Alex feigned a smile.

"You sure? Cause you have been kind of distant. Things good with Amir?" Kim asked.

"Definitely," Alex smiled again, taking a sip from her glass. Tonight, was one she wasn't looking forward to. It was their monthly check-in. It usually took place during the middle of the month. However, if they were too busy, it was moved. But with her and Amir in town, it was inevitable.

"Keisha's right though. You do have a glow. Saw you moving that ass more than usual when you walked right in," Rita added with a grin.

Alex laughed. For awhile, she had felt insecure about her sexuality. But Jay had made her realize there was nothing wrong about her. She was normal, just with more of a sexual crave. This knowledge had made her more confident. The pleasures, orgasms, and the heights he had taken her to made her embrace her sexuality and her body. And it was a beautiful realization she was definitely owning.

"I'm so sorry I'm late," Nancy said, hurrying in. "Amanda dropped by, and I had to spend hours consoling her."

Amanda was the wife of celebrity basketball player, Tristan. They had been high school sweethearts who had gotten married in college. They had like a team of children, with Amanda popping out one every other year. She was totally in love with him, however Tristan had a wandering eye. His infidelity was usually covered up, and even Alex never revealed the many times he tried to hit on her.

"What? Some side chick sent her pictures of her man?" Keisha asked.

"No, Tristan is expecting a child with that Monae chick. You know the Instagram influencer," Nancy said.

"Instagram thot!" Keisha corrected.

Alex agreed with her. She had visited her page one time – actually stumbled on it because it had been suggested – and all she had seen were booty pictures. All she was marketing was her vagina and nothing else. Monae was associated with almost every man out there. How could Tristan have gone that low?

"He's stupid. What was he thinking? Monae, of all bitches? That thot would screw in the dumpster for $5," Rita said shaking her head.

"She's so devastated. I'm so worried about her. Shit hasn't hit the news yet, but Monae isn't going to get rid of that baby, and she wants child support. In the millions," Nancy said.

"What's Tristan saying about this mess?" Kim asked.

Nancy rolled her eyes. "The asshole said Monae trapped him. I can't believe he slept with her without protection. You know how many diseases are walking out there? These men ain't loyal! They ain't worth it!"

"I told y'all that long ago. That's why I screw whoever I want, no commitments. The world can call me names, but I can't sit around with my arms folded while my man dips off on me with anybody that comes his way. Play me, I don't think so," Keisha said with a self-toast.

*

Alex returned home with thoughts. She wondered if in their years of marriage Amir had cheated on her. It was said that men could not be faithful, and the ones that acted faithful hid their affairs well. However, she trusted Amir, but still, was he capable of cheating? She never would have imagined that she, brought up in a strict Baptist home, a woman of values would cheat on her husband, but she had. Didn't that mean that Amir could do the same as well? Alex knew she was just trying to justify her actions, but there was doubt in her mind. If Amir had cheated on her, then she was doing nothing wrong. But if he hadn't? If he had remained true to her? Did that thought make her feel guilty? Yes, did it. At times she lay in bed, eyes closed, but awake, thinking of what she was doing, but the pleasure and excitement always overrode those feelings.

Amir was already home. Waiting. He had changed out of his suit to a comfy T-shirt and shorts. He was ready for their monthly check-in. The idea had occurred to him while watching a popular movie where a black couple had gone to see a therapist. In front of the therapist, they had admitted what was wrong with their marriage and to each other's surprise, neither had been aware of what the other was feeling. And then Amir had a thought. Instead of going to see a therapist, why not just talk it out? Why not act like therapists and address the problems themselves, instead of adding in a complete stranger? He had brought the idea to Alex and she had been cool with it. They had met monthly for the past three years. While he was honest, he felt she was holding back most times. Perhaps it was fear of hurting him, but he was not as fragile as she thought he was. He could take on anything. He loved her no matter what, and always open to working on making their marriage a success.

Alex joined him in his office, where their meetings held – in a formal setting. It was a serious setting because marriage is serious business. There were no food or drinks that could cause distractions, just bottles of water. She settled on the couch opposite him. Inside, she was a bumbling mess. There was so much she wanted to say. But saying them would destroy him.

"How was your day?" Amir asked.

"Eventful. Lots of meetings, and dinner with the girls. How was the meeting with Griffin?" she asked. Griffin was an old friend, who now lived in London, and was in town for a movie.

"Griffin is doing great. He has lost a lot of pounds, and has never been better. Jay stopped by. I had to wrap things up with him in haste, so he wouldn't interfere with our time," Amir said. He liked the kid no doubt, and although he was welcome to his home, he hadn't expected him to take advantage of it to this extent. He stopped by a lot. Even for reasons that could be quickly resolved over a call. Maybe Jay was just wanting to prove to Amir how eager he was to learn, he reasoned.

"Oh, how are things going with him?"

"Slow, but great. Shooting for Seun's show starts next week, but I want to get him on that medical series Holland directs. Put him out there into a medical scene," Amir said. According to Jay, he had been watching and studying medical series since he was a kid, and had always dreamed of starring in one. While expertise was great in being an actor, he wanted Jay to be versatile; he was too young to start playing a certain role, which could be attached to him forever. That was what made a good actor, versatility.

They went around in circles, before moving past the ice-breaking phase. Amir went straight to what he had observed in the last month. "I feel that you have become distant from me. I wanted to talk about it last month, but I wasn't sure, but now I am."

"Distant in what sense?" Alex asked, masking a slight attitude.

"You are here, but not here. Especially intimately. When we make love, it seems like you are elsewhere. Like you are thinking of someone else when we have sex." Sounded as if this had been worrying him for a while now. Their sex-life had become cold, colder. She moaned and was responsive, but he knew this woman. He had been married to her for five years now, and he knew when something was different. The way she looked at him. The way her body responded to him. He had always felt her holding back, but this time it was different. It was like she just wanted it to be over with. It was like she wasn't there in the moment. It was just a bit of everything.

Alex laughed nervously.

"I'm serious, Alex. You have fantasies, right? Who are in your fantasies?" Amir asked.

"I don't have fantasies. You are the one I think of when we have sex," Alex smiled.

He knew she was lying. At times he just wanted her to stop holding back, and to be free and honest with him. There were moments when Amir stared at her, realizing he really didn't know her. And he wanted to know her. Everything about her. Her desires. Her fantasies. He wants. Her needs. Her secrets. They might be scandalous, but he didn't care. He would accept them.

"Alex, please just tell me. I won't be angry. I just want to know so we can figure out a way to spice up our sexual life. We can throw things out, and add in new things," Amir pleaded.

"Amir, I don't think of anyone else when I am with you. Maybe I am just tired, or you are reading me the wrong way. You are the only one I think of. You are more than enough for me Amir, and you shouldn't let your insecurities get the best of you," Alex responded. However, she knew that Amir was still holding on to his beliefs. The man could be so damn stubborn! Did he really expect her to tell him her fantasies? That she loved being spanked? That she would like to be fucked in the ass while a dildo fucked her pussy? That she liked being tied up by Jay with a blind over her eyes? He would probably drop from a heart attack!

Amir got off the couch and came to her, taking her hand in his, and staring at her tenderly. "Alex, there's nothing you can tell me that will make me angry. I love you, and no matter what I am ready to make this marriage work."

He always said this, but would he keep to his words if she told him the truth? Men had such fragile egos. They were like babies, who would switch characters when told the truth.

"Amir, I think of no one but you. Work is crazy but…"

"But what?" Amir asked. He knew there was something she wanted to tell him.

Alex sighed. He wasn't going to relent unless she gave him something. "I'm scared you are going to leave me, Amir."

Amir pulled away from her, with a frown. "What are you talking about? Why would I do some shit like that?"

"Because I can't give you what you want. Children," Alex said, telling him the truth but definitely not being completely honest. Yes, she was upset that she couldn't have children, but she had accepted her fate a long time ago, way back when she was a teenager. However, it was one of the reasons she had been unable to settle down. Most men wanted children and had been unable to deal with her infertility. Despite the quick timeframe within which she and Amir had met and gotten married, she had deliberately kept that knowledge from him. Because she was sure he would walk away and not marry her. It had been selfish of her, but she had known Amir was a great catch, and she would never come across a man like him again. A responsible black man who honored the sanctity of marriage was hard to find not just in the industry, but in the world.

"I..." Amir was shocked. He had never thought she felt that way. "You think I am going to leave you?"

Alex nodded.

"But I told you I don't care... well, as much as I want to have kids, if they are not with you...forget it. I have accepted the way things are," he reassured her.

Alex scoffed. "That's what you say, but someday you're gonna realize that you really want kids, and you're going to replace me." Despite him being a responsible husband, it was a possibility she had thought of. Many men took that path when their wives were unable to conceive. She really didn't use to worry, because she trusted Amir, but then she had trusted herself too. And as much as it would hurt her, she would not blame him for wanting to procreate. However, having a child outside of the marriage came with some major issues. And she didn't want some skinny bitch chatting her up on Instagram, because she would go down swinging. There was already a lot going on in her life and she had no room for drama.

"No. I ain't gonna do that. Hell no!" Amir exclaimed ensuring he removed any doubt in her mind. Had the thought occurred to him? Hell yes! A couple of his friends had suggested that he get himself a side-chick and have at least one child. He even had a cousin who had brought his outside child home and the kid was being cared for by his wife. But he wasn't down for that type of shit. He wouldn't let his desire for a child open up ways to ruin his marriage. And after over twenty years of being in Hollywood, he had seen how baby mamas destroyed marriages. Most of them weren't comfortable with child support and their bills getting paid. They wanted a ring and a surname. They wanted to spite the legally married wife. They brought with them all sort of drama that would make a man spend years in court fighting legal battles. Hate would grow between the parents, and the children would suffer the consequences.

"Alex," he turned her face to his, and stared into her eyes. "I promise you, just like I did the day we took our vows before God, that I'm not quitting on this marriage nor going to hurt you. And I'm definitely not going to step out on you. Never. You are my wife, and we ride together, no matter what. Understand?"

Alex nodded. "I just... I want you to have a child, Amir. I want to have kids, and it really drives me crazy that we don't have any. I mean we got all this money, and shit, and we don't have anyone to share it with."

"Then let's find alternate ways. I know we talked about adoption and surrogacy in the past, but we were always too distracted to follow through. Let's get serious about this shit now. Talk to some doctors. Know what our options are. We're gonna have children, you'll see," Amir added with a smile.

Alex chuckled. He was right. This time around they needed to take this seriously. They were drawing close to 50, and she didn't want to have a kid in diapers when she was sixty. Let's call the doctor, first thing tomorrow," Alex said.

"We're going to do this, we going to have the family we want. We. Together, Alex. I mean my words. We are not going to be like my parents. We are going to have a happy home. We are blessed, baby. We are blessed," Amir said, kissing her knuckles.

"Yeah, we are blessed," Alex sighed. And just like that, Amir had let go of the idea he had of her fantasizing about another man. But she knew if she continued to be distant, the idea was going to pop back in again. She just needed to get control of the situation. Be in the present, and stop letting Jay take over her thoughts. It was going to be damn hard, but she wasn't an award-winning actress for nothing.

CHAPTER ELEVEN

A laugh bubbled up from Alex's throat as Jay wiggled his waist in tune with the song coming from his phone. He was a good dancer, and she was turned on, just watching him strip. She gestured at him to join her on the bed, but he just winked at her, as his shorts came off. Her tongue instinctively licked her lips at the sight of his erection.

"Jay! Get your ass over here!" she instructed. She wanted him right now.

Jay chuckled as he made his way to her in quick strides. She was breathtaking in a red corset which lifted the breasts his hands ached to play with. But not yet. He had a lot of surprises for her.

"You are too much in a hurry. We got the whole day to ourselves," Jay said. Amir was out of town, which meant he was spending the night over. Stroking that yoni in every position he could think of.

"Well, I don't have time to waste," Alex said, reaching for him.

Amir grabbed her hands and she squealed, throwing him a dirty look. "What do you think you are doing?"

He pulled her to him. "You want this dick so bad, don't you? Close your eyes," he whispered.

"Yes," Alex moaned while obeying his command. She wanted it more than he knew. Her eyes flung open as she felt a cloth around her wrists. "Jay! What the hell do you think you are doing?" He was tying her wrists with a scarf. She tried to get loose but the knot was too tight.

"Wanted to do that since the first day I set my eyes on you," Jay revealed as she continued to struggle.

"Jay, untie this shit!" her nose flared. They had done some light BDSM, spanking, biting, but they had never gone this far.

"Not yet." He pulled her to him once again.

Alex was so distracted with trying to get out of the wrist restraints that she didn't see the blind coming over her eyes until it was too late.

"Jay!" she snapped. She wasn't down for shit like that. She wanted to see her partner while she was being stroked. Being blind-folded made her vulnerable, and a little frightened.

"Alex," Jay said, placing a finger over her lips. "Don't be scared. I won't hurt you. You trust me, right?"

She took a deep breath, and realized she did. Yes, she trusted him. Alex nodded.

"You're going to have a good time," Jay said, pushing her on the bed.

She had never felt so powerless as she was, laying down on the bed, her hands tied, and her eyes blinded. What was he up to? Everything seemed more sensitive than before. She could hear the distant honks. The creaks on the bed made her alert. What plans did he—

Alex went still as his warm hands caressed her feet. His touch was gentle and made her sleepy. His magical hands made her moan as she imagined those slick flingers sliding into her, one finger at a time, coating her with her essence.

Alex jolted at his hot breath, as he sucked on her toe. It sent signals straight to her dripping pussy. His kiss moved higher, with him kissing her legs, taking his time to caress her. She remained still, basking in pleasure, waiting for him to get between her moist thighs. She moaned as he caressed her slit through her panties.

"Jaaayyyy," she cried as he pushed her wet panties aside momentarily then let go. Suddenly, the bed creaked, and she felt him get off of it. Where was he going? "Jay?" she called to him.

She was a beautiful sight. The most beautiful he had ever seen. He wanted to take a picture of her, he could always look at. And as much as he wanted to reach for his phone and take pictures, she trusted him, and he wouldn't ruin that trust. For now, this image of her, with her arms tied, with her powerless to his control would be ingrained in his memory. Forever.

"Jay?" Alex called out again, turning on the bed, hopefully in the direction he disappeared in.

Jay, standing near the bedroom door trifle through his luggage looking for his smaller "special bag". After locating his treasure, he went back to the bed.

"Jay, I don't have time for jokes. You know I hate like horror movies, and this seems like something straight out of one," Alex pouted.

Jay laughed a little then her down with both hands as he slid her panty off her, tossing it to the ground.

"What the—" Alex cried in surprise as something other than Jay's dick, tongue or fingers slid into her pussy.

It was then she realized what it was. A vibrator. Set to the lowest. Her mouth widened as she groaned louder and louder. It was pure torture yet pleasure. She wanted him to turn the speed up. And even worse Jay was teasing her, whirling that thing between her legs, pulling away every time she thrust her body, begging for more.

Jay grinned, watching her turned on face. She was so freaking turned on, with her pussy glistening. "What do you want?" Jay asked, stroking his dick.

"Turn it up faster!" Alex cried.

He grazed her with the vibrator as he increased the speed. Alex thrashed on the bed as he pulled the vibrator away from her. She was going to make him pay for this torture. She was going to tie him down and sit on his dick without moving. Only when he begged would she ride that dick.

Her eyes squeezed tightly when Jay finally thrusted the vibrator into her again. The fast tempo made her cry out as she struggled against the bound. She needed something to hold on to. The sheets. His body. Anything! Jay moving that pulsating wand from inside of her to her throbbing clit made her climax, almost against her will. Her body rose and fell back on the bed, breathing softly. She moaned as he kissed her, his naked body brushing against her. She tried to reach for him as he teased her flooded hole with his erection. He knew she wanted him now in the worse way.

"Jayyyy, Jayyyy," she cried out. She couldn't hold it any longer. Her scream was swallowed by Jay, as he kissed her deeply. Just as she was recuperating, his dick slid into her. It hit all her senses as she struggled to free her hands, wanting to touch him so bad, more than ever before.

Jay panted as he sucked hard on her nipple, stroking her hot tightness. She was a drug he wanted more of. He was addicted to her scent, her taste, her warmth. Everything! She took his rod like she was made for him. Her cries made him grow harder as he pounded into her.

Tears rolled down her face as Jay indulged in her. He drove harder and harder into her and she exploded, seeing stars. His dick stiffened in her as he came with a loud roar, his body resting on her as he took deep breaths.

"Get this off me," Alex whispered tiredly.

She was happy when the restraints came off so she could caress him. Even happier when the blind-fold came off and she could stare into his eyes. Her heart twitched as he stared back. The intimacy she felt, and saw in his eyes scared her.

Jay kissed her. "I love you, Alex." He had been aching to tell her those words. And could not hold them back anymore.

"You love me?" Alex asked, stunned.

"Yes, I do. And I know you might not have a response right now but I'm sure—"

Alex froze at a sound. It was the intercom. Someone was at the gate. They shared a look.

"Are you expecting someone?" Jay asked.

"No," Alex replied carelessly.

"Leave it," Jay said, as his fingers found her clit. "I love stroking you and—"

Her phone rang, causing her eyes to snap open.

"Leave it," Jay said, while trying to caress her hardened nub to ecstasy.

"I... I... It could be... It could be Amir," Alex said. She grabbed her phone and answered it. "Hello?" she asked breathlessly as Jay kissed her neck, his fingers still slow dancing with her clitoris.

"Alex, I am at your gate," Kim said.

Alex sat up straight, pushing Jay away. "What? Where you say you at?"

"Your gate. Rang the bell like five times. Are you home?" Kim asked.

"Umm... yeah. I will let you in now," Alex said as she grabbed her black satin robe.

"Who the hell is that?" Jay asked with a glare. The whole day was supposed to be for him and Alex. Who the hell was interrupting their moment?

"My friend, Kim. This won't take long at all. I will be fast," Alex said, hurrying to the bathroom and grabbing a brush which she ran through her hair. "Stay put, no noise," she warned, giving him a quick kiss before running out the door. As she hurried down, she was indeed glad for the interruption.

Jay tossed a pillow as the door shut closed.

"Kim!" Alex said in a highly pitched voice as the door opened, with Kim walking in.

"Are you okay?" Kim asked, with a lifted brow.

"Sure, sure," Alex said, taking deep breaths. Her heart pounded with the excitement of orgasms and now entertaining her friend. And the thought of having a dirty little secret up in the bedroom, right above Kim's head, increased the intensity of her excitement.

"I was about to head back home, I thought you weren't here," Kim said.

"Oh. I was upstairs. Resting," Alex lied.

"At two in the afternoon?" Kim asked with an eyeroll. "Anyway, I thought of checking up on you. I haven't seen you in a while."

"Yeah... been busy with stuff," Alex yawned.

"Is it work or the baby thing?"

She had shared with her friends, except Keisha about her and Amir plans to have a child. Amir was spending a lot of time doing research. His office was filled with pamphlets given to them by the doctor who had given them hope that they could have their own child. On her part however, she wasn't that excited. Yes, she would love to have a child, but having an affair didn't make it all that exciting. Bringing a child into the equation just didn't seem fair, but Amir was excited, and she couldn't rain on his parade.

"A mix of both, I guess. How's everyone at home? Want something to drink? A beer? Wine?"

"I'll take a beer," Kim said, following her to the kitchen.

"Are you going to Keisha's thing?" Alex asked, as she placed a bottle of beer in front of Kim.

"Keisha's thing?" Kim laughed.

Keisha's birthday was in a week, and sure enough she was throwing a crazy party. Parties with Keisha were always over the top, and this was not going to be any different. Usually, Alex popped in for a few minutes and she was out before the drugs and other craziness followed. It was going to be no different this time around. Because if she didn't drop by, Keisha was going to hold a grudge against her for a long time.

"I don't know why she can't just have an intimate dinner. Most of the guests don't give a shit about her," Alex said.

"You know Keisha. That bitch is loud, obnoxious and wouldn't be happy if she didn't act a fool every time she throws a party. We sure got a crazy friend. Tell me again why we associate with her," Kim joked.

"I tell you. I don't even know what to get as a gift. You know how picky she can be," Alex said.

"Damn! Forgot about a gift, she was gonna—" A sound came from upstairs.

"Is someone else here?" Kim asked, glancing toward the winding staircase.

"It should be the housekeeper," Alex said.

"Oh," Kim said, but she could see her friend didn't believe her.

Kim didn't stay around long after that. She made up some excuse and was on her way, with Alex wearing her signature smile and waving her 'good-bye". She knew Kim. There wouldn't definitely be an impromptu quiz at a later date. And Alex's answers had better be foolproof.

Jay was scrolling through his phone, naked on the bed when she returned. She glared at him, swatting him with a pillow.

"What?" he asked, jumping.

"You made a noise. I was supposed to be home alone." Alex said.

"Sorry babe, but you have no idea how bored I was, just being up here alone. I wanted to bring my ass downstairs, and show your friend what you enjoying," Jay grinned as he dodged another pillow Alex had thrown.

She glared at him playfully, a smile itching. He pulled her to him and she kissed him. As her hands caressed his back, she joined him in the bed. Then almost as if someone was adjusting a dimmer switch, her eyes began closing, body began to relaxing, and slumber had its way with her.

*

Alex was fast asleep when Jay eased out of the bed. He spared her a look just to be sure, but even then she wouldn't suspect anything. He wore his shorts and grabbed his wallet, then closed the door quietly behind him.

Downstairs, Jay stopped in front of an artwork which was worth at least a million. He always admired it. This house had become a second home to him so much so that he could walk around in the dark, with the lights off without bumping into anything. When he left, back to his scrawny apartment, a part of him was always left behind here. He whistled softly as he approached Amir's office. As expected, it was unlocked.

Amir's office was cool, with dark wood and décor. It reeked of masculinity. The shelves were filled with books which Alex said Amir had read. All of them. She had said it with pride, as if reading was some dope shit. Jay wasn't fond of books. He had read all kinds of bullshit in school and was done with it.

He sat on the leather armchair, resting his legs on the table. He smiled as he looked around. He had taken several pictures of himself in this office, but he couldn't upload them on the Gram. At least not yet. But soon he would. When the office became his.

A sound in a distance reminded him of the task at hand. Now was not the time to be relaxing. He went to one of the shelves and reached for the bottle of cognac. It was Amir's favorite, which he had told him the first day he came here. No one but Amir drank from it. It was his special signature brew. And he sure loved his cognac, especially on weekends.

Jay removed a sachet of white powder from his wallet and filtered it into the bottle of brown liquid, shaking it around to ensure it dissolved. Then he carefully placed the bottle back on the shelf. He hesitated by the door to the office with a menacing grin. Then he returned to the bedroom, and slid in next to his woman on the bed. Cuddling up to Alex, he joined her in some well needed sleep.

CHAPTER TWELVE

The party was in full swing when the Sheldons arrived. Keisha had allowed a few reporters on the grounds, but they would be escorted out before the "real party" fully kicked off. Phones of the guests would also be confiscated so no one could record what went down. Although there was always that one person who was able to get away and leak pictures and info to the press.

Keisha had gone with a circus theme, with clowns, dancers, and magicians making a ruckus. Amir shook his head. He would rather celebrate his birthday with people who truly cared about him. And not with this charade that would cause headaches later on.

"I know that face, but don't worry, we will be out in about an hour," Alex said.

"An hour seems like a pretty long time," Amir replied, as a headache suddenly hit him. He winced at the pain.

"Are you okay?" Alex asked.

"Yes. Just a headache. Probably the noise and crowd," Amir said. He knew he was due to seeing the doctor, but he was just too busy with work. The headaches had started a few weeks ago, usually followed by brief nausea. They barely occurred when he was out of town, but when he returned home, they swooped in hard on him.

"Let's go say hello to our hostess," Alex said, directing her husband towards Keisha who wore a glittery silver gown, with her hair pinned up. She looked great, with her recent BBL, which was a birthday gift from herself.

"Alex! Amir! My favorite couple!" Keisha said in excitement. She was either drunk or high, as she grabbed Alex.

"Happy birthday, Keisha. You sure threw a big one this year," Amir said.

Keisha laughed happily. "You know me. Ain't no party like a Keisha-party. Where is my gift at Alex? Don't tell me you brought that ass of yours empty-handed?"

Alex reached in her Birkin handbag. "I got you this," she said, handing her a box of Tiffany stud earrings.

Keisha gleamed with excitement when she looked at the content. Then she crushed Alex with a hug. "You and Amir deserve some wild fun tonight! You up for a threesome, Amir?"

"I'll pass. We are going to find some place to sit," Amir said, escaping with his wife in tow.

"An hour maybe too long, I think we will be gone in thirty minutes," Alex smiled. However, her smile wasn't returned. She followed Amir's gaze and gasped. Jay was here as well. What the hell was he doing here? Then she reminded herself. This was Atlanta and of course he would be here now that he and Amir had some of the same connections.

"What's he doing here?" Amir asked, taking a glass from a waiter.

"Umm... this is Atlanta? Is everything okay?" She had noticed that Amir wasn't as enthusiastic about Jay as he had been months ago. Did he suspect that she was fucking Jay? But if he did, surely he would have done something…said something. And he would have confronted her during their monthly check-ups.

"I… I think Jay likes me," Amir finally said. And it did sound awkward.

"Of course, he does. Why would he hate you?" Alex asked with a forced laugh then accepted a glass of wine from the waiter and sipped it. Just at times, the way Jay talked about being with her, the way he excluded Amir scared her. Just at times. But she guessed it was jealousy. He was doing a lot of talking about wanting her for himself nowadays. He wasn't satisfied with the stolen moments they had. He wanted more. He wanted a whole damn relationship. And she was a married woman.

"I don't mean that kind of like. I mean like like," Amir said.

Her eyes widened in realization. She almost spat the wine out of her mouth. Then she burst into a laugh. "You think Jay is gay? That he likes you in a sexual kind of way?" Jay was going to laugh his ass off when she told him this.

"Yes, and it's not funny. It is like he always wants to be around me. I mean I am cool with mentoring the kid and all that. But it is like he bombards my life. I see him pop up everywhere. You know the other day I saw him at the golf club. And a few weeks back he was at that meeting I went to downtown. He ran into me and said he was in the neighborhood. Then he drops by the house so randomly. I know I said he's welcome to our home anytime, but I didn't expect him to take that shit literally. I just don't feel cool with it. It is uncomfortable. And it all adds up to one thing,"

Amir continued. He had tried to put it off, and come up with excuses, but it was becoming clear to him. Jay had feelings for him. It was why he wanted to be around in the house all the time. Now, he had no problem with shit like that. But not when it unsettled him in a way he couldn't describe.

The kid had some real talent, but now he wasn't sure he was the person who could help him polish and enhance it. Besides, he had come to realize that Jay was smooth and full of shit. He was the type of person who was willing to cut corners to get to where he wanted. And people like that could be dangerous. He had heard from someone who had seen him with Jay, that Jay slept around for favors. And with how Atlanta worked, these could include men, which explained why Jay had a crush on him. But he wasn't interested by any means.

Now, he was in no place to judge people, but he had principles he worked with, and he didn't compromise them. He and Jay just didn't have the chemistry to work together anymore. He had built his fame and wealth on hard work, and Jay didn't seem like someone willing to do that work. When they had met, Jay had portrayed a different character to him but now someone else was unfolding.

Amir was going to have to cut him loose eventually. But he would try to help him, at least until then because he had made a commitment. In the meantime, he was going to give him some distance.

"I don't think Jay likes you that way, honey" Alex said.

"Why?"

"I think he likes women," Alex noted.

Amir scoffed. "I don't think so. I have never seen him show an interest in a woman. None at all. It is like he doesn't even see them. I have also not heard a woman call him, or him call a woman." His words made him become even more suspicious of Jay having feelings for him. He was young, and good looking, and women had flirted with him in his presence, but Jay never reciprocated.

"Maybe he has a girlfriend that he's faithful to," Alex suggested.

Indeed. Amir was going to go with his theory. "He's headed this way," Amir whispered over his glass.

"Amir! Alex!" Jay said with a huge grin. He had known Alex would attend the party and had gotten himself on the guest list just to be with her.

"Jay, fancy meeting you here. I didn't know you hung around this crowd," Amir said.

Jay chuckled. There was no crowd he couldn't get in. You just needed to know the right people. "You guys look great," Jay said, ignoring Amir's statement but checking him out from head to toe.

Amir threw his wife a look, hoping she had seen howe Jay was admiring him.

Suddenly, Amir winced as he went blind for a moment. Alex held on to him with concern. "Are you okay?"

"Yes, I need to step outside for a moment. I will be back," Amir said, excusing himself.

Jay watched him leave. The concoction was taking effect. Slowly, but surely. The idea had occurred to him while watching one of his medical dramas. Amir was a stumbling block that hindered him from having Alex all to himself. She didn't love Amir any way, but she had some sense of responsibility to him. And worse, Amir wanted to have kids. He needed to step in before Alex made the mistake of having children with him. The only man she was allowed to have kids with was him.

"What are you doing here?" Alex hissed.

"It is a free world, sweetheart," Jay chuckled.

Alex shook her head, and threw him a warning look. "Don't try anything stupid!" The party was crowded, but there were eyes watching.

"What do you mean by stupid?" Jay leaned in with a whisper.

She pulled away from him. "I have to check on Amir. Have fun."

Jay grabbed a glass of scotch from a passing waiter, then tossed it back into his mouth as if it was nothing but water. His mood worsened when he saw Amir return, taking Alex to the dancefloor. He hated seeing that man with her. Seeing his hands on her skin. Seeing him kiss her. It was supposed to be him! He was the one who should have Alex in his arms. He should show her to the world, let them know she was his woman, and he her man.

It drove him nuts! He fought the urge to go over there and pull Amir away, smash him in the face until his body went still. But he was going to be patient. If there was something he had learned, wars weren't always won by physical battles.

*

Alex's eyes closed as Amir planted a kiss on her neck. Her gown was bunched at her waist, as he sucked her breasts. She imagined he was Jay, with his well-toned youthful body. She wished he would lift her up like she weighed nothing, then throw her on the bed, and thrust that hard dick of his into her.

"Alex?"

Her eyes opened and she stared at her husband. "Yes?" she asked in a whisper.

"Are you okay?" Amir asked tiredly.

"Yes. Are you? You seem really tired," Alex said.

He pulled away from her. He did feel tired. He didn't have much work these days, so was usually in bed early, hence it was a surprise he still felt tired. The tiredness came with crazy headaches and nausea, and a few days ago, blood had come from his nose. Alex was not aware of his symptoms. He was scared but he was going to blame it on stress. He wasn't going to think of anything else. He was a fit man. He ate right. He exercised. He didn't smoke. But he did drink, especially his cognac which he drank regularly.

"I do feel tired," Amir said, laying on the bed.

"You should go to the doctor tomorrow," Alex replied with concern. The room was well ventilated but sweat had gathered on his forehead.

"I should. I just need to take a rest," Amir said as he adjusted on the bed. In a few minutes, he was fast asleep, and she watched him with concern- wondering what was wrong. Amir rarely got sick, and when he did, he quickly bounced back.

Alexandria's phone buzzed. It was Jay. She had saved his number with a female name, and her messages with him were encrypted. She had thought of putting a lock on her phone, but that would quickly notify Amir that she was up to something.

Jay: I miss you.

Alex: I miss you too.

The old Alex would judge women like her. Women who cheated on their husbands, and worse of all with a man young enough to be her son. But life had taught her a lot of lessons. Jay said he was in love with her; he didn't hesitate telling her that he loved her. But on her part, she had never returned the words. She found him adorable and had a special fondness for him. But love? No, she didn't love him. With Jay, there was a youthful exuberance. He made her feel alive, he made her feel special and confident. She still loved her husband. Very much.

Things with Jay were becoming quite serious. Too serious. More than she had anticipated. He was making demands of her. He wanted to go out with her in public. He wanted her to sleep over. He had even suggested her divorcing Amir. He promised her a lifetime of happiness. That he would always be there for her. He whispered sweet words into her ears, and at times, she let herself share those dreams of his. She imagined the both of them together happy, starting afresh. But those dreams soon faded as reality dawned on her. She would be fifty in a few years, and he would be thirty! For now, he claimed to love her, but eventually, as they grew older, he would turn his attention elsewhere, to a younger woman. It was inevitable. Besides, hurting Amir publicly? It would ruin him not only if she ended things with him, but started dating his mentee? Throw in the media backlash she would receive. Things with Jay were fun, there was no doubt about that, but he was silly to assume that she was going to leave her husband for him. He knew what they were doing when they got involved. It was an affair. An entanglement.

She took a deep breath as she realized the mess she had gotten into. She was scared of how it was going to end. She could still end it with Jay. But she couldn't force herself to do so. She couldn't hurt him, he cared for her. He had a young and free heart, and her hurting him might just turn him cold towards other women. And besides, she wasn't ready to lose what she had with him. Her marriage was boring as hell, she couldn't recall the last time she had good sex with Amir. Blame it on the great sex she had with Jay, but sex with Amir was like eating hot salad. She didn't look forward to it, but still sexed him out of obligation.

Jay: Are you home alone?

Alex: No, Amir is here. He's under the weather.

Jay grimaced on the other side of town, staring at his screen. This shit was taking too long. He was going to have to up the dosage, to get Amir out of the way. He was getting frustrated with Alex's inability to make a choice. She had tried to make him see things from her point of view. How he was too young for her. But he didn't care. He loved her, and was going to be with her till when he was old and grey. Then about her bullshit respect for her husband. Out of sentiment, Alex was not going to leave Amir, but he had taken care of it. With Amir out of the way, he would step in and be a support to the mourning Alex. Then, no one would be able to stand in their way.

The media would go crazy about their union. He grinned as he thought of it. Of the articles that would follow when they announced their relationship. All hell would definitely break loose. They would be crucified by the press, but he didn't care about them. Some other shit would happen and they would leave them alone. He would have the woman he loved, and well, the wealth that followed would be a welcome and added bonus.

CHAPTER THIRTEEN

It felt good, the way his hands caressed her ass. She had been fucked in her ass a couple of times, but it wasn't something she actually liked as those men had not been gentle, probably lost in the pleasure of pumping an ass so tight. But with Jay she knew it was going to be different. He had always hinted at it, and today was that day. And she was ready. She had been imagining it for a while, and had found herself playing with her asshole. She had even tried penetrating herself with a dildo, anticipating this very day.

"Have I told you that you got the best ass ever?" Jay asked, pulling her ass closer to his cock.

"You tell me every time," Alex said, writhing against him.

"I just love seeing it," Jay said with excitement, squeezing her ass.

"You want to go in it? It is all yours," Alex said.

"You mean it?"

She chuckled at the excitement in his voice. "Hell yeah!" He hugged her, pressing his dick against her. Her pussy grew wet as he began to kiss her neck, his kiss going lower on her back. Then he grabbed her ass, squeezing it tight as he dropped a kiss on her cheek.

All humor disappeared, as her body clenched in anticipation. "Jay?" she whispered. His finger was in her crack now. At her entrance. Teasing. Playing. He was quiet. And then she felt it. His tongue slid in as he spread her ass wide open.

"Oh. Oh…" Words failed her as she spoke intelligibly. It was dirty! No one had stuck his tongue into her ass. But it felt so damn good. It was the best feeling ever. She grabbed the sheet, twisting, until he pinned her down, his tongue sliding deeper as he ate her ass.

"Oh my.. oh my.." Her eyes rolled to the back. This was an experience she would definitely not forget. An experience she wanted a repeat of! If she had known it would feel this way, she would have done it a long time ago! However, only a few men would— All thoughts disappeared as his thumb slid into her ass, his other fingers caressing her now swollen clitoris.

"Alexxxx," Jay groaned, as he entered another finger into her ass. He watched in amazement as he finger-fucked her ass. It too becoming moist. This woman was paradise. Ain't no way someone could tell him different.

The bed dipped as Jay got off the bed. She wondered where he had gone to, when he quickly returned with a lube of Vaseline from the bathroom. She gasped at the coldness of the cream as he spread it all over her crack.

"Grab a condom for me!" he mumbled.

Her hands shaking, she reached for the packet of condom on the bedside table and tore the sheet, handing it over to him.

He was hard as a rock. The dick couldn't wait to penetrate her asshole. Especially knowing he got there before Amir who grimaced at the mention of the asshole. He shook off the thought of Amir. Not now, when he was with his woman.

"Are you ready, baby?" Jay groaned, turning her on her side. He knew it was going to hurt, but she was going to love it.

Tears came to Alex's eyes as he slid into her. It was so painful His dick pushed deeper into her and she cried out in pain. "Get it out!"

"Am sorry babe. It is gonna hurt at first, but it will be good to you. Please?" Jay begged, reaching over and sliding his fingers back into her pussy.

It was a distraction for her, fucking her pussy as he slid deeper into her ass. Despite the air conditioning in the room, he was sweating. Her ass was so freakin tight but it was where he wanted to be. And then he began to move, slowly.

Alex moaned as the pain consumed her, and at the same time with pleasure. It was different from anything she had felt. She wanted it to stop, but at the same time, she wanted it to continue.

"Jayyyyyy, deeper," she begged, squeezing her breasts.

Jay wanted to give it to her harder, but he didn't want to hurt her, so he pulled out of her gently, thrusting back into her harder. The sound of skin slapping against skin, with moans and grunts filled the room.

"Fuckkkkkk!" Jay let loose as he exploded in that tight ass.

Alex wasn't far behind. "What the hell are you doing to meeeee?" Alex yelled at the top of her voice before both her pussy and ass detonated in one body shaking explosion.

She remained in that position, weak, breathing softly. "Pull out!" she said, feeling the burning pain again.

She curled up on the bed as Jay went to the bathroom to get rid of the condom. Damn, that had been intense, and although she wanted a repeat, not anytime soon. Her eyes were about closing, when a buzz pulled her from sleep. It was the house phone ringing.

"Leave it babe," Jay said, jumping back into the bed to get some sleep.

"No one calls the house phone. Must be important," Alex said, getting out of bed. Deciding to take the call in privacy, she grabbed her robe and went downstairs. She caught the ringing before it ended.

"Why are you not picking up your fucking phone!" Chris yelled. He was one of Amir's close friends, and they were on a set downtown together for the rest of the day.

"Chris... I didn't know you called." Her phone had been right beside her. She would have heard it ring.

"I have called you over ten times. Everyone has!"

"Chris, what is going on?" Alex asked, voice showing concern.

"Amir is in the hospital."

The phone slid out of her hand.

"Alex? Alex you there? What the fuck?"

She quickly grabbed the phone. "What do you mean Amir is in the hospital? You kidding me or what?"

"Why the fuck would I do that? We were on set and he just fucking collapsed. We called an ambulance and they took him to the hospital. We are here now and none of those fucking doctors have come the fuck out to tell us what's happening. Am about to lose my fucking mind!"

"I am on my way. Right now!"

Jay was about to go get Alex when the door flew open, with her running to the closet. He followed her naked, his dick swinging.

"Where the fire at?" he teased.

"Amir is at the hospital!" Alex cried, as she grabbed a black blouse and some jeans.

"Oh. What happened to him?"

"I don't know! I don't know! I need to go be with him, I am sorry Jay, I just…"

He hugged her. "It is gonna be okay. Probably stress or shit like that," he reassured her.

"Yeah, yeah. Could you help me…" She looked around the room. It was quite a mess.

"Don't worry I will. I'll call you later," Jay said, with a kiss.

Alex nodded as she grabbed her purse, before running out the room. He watched her from the window as she drove off, then he did a little victory dance. Amir was in the hospital, and it was just a matter of time before the prick was dead. The asshole had the guts to tell him that he couldn't work with him! Screw him! He thought he was better than him. He thought because he had money he could look the fuck down at him? He had told Jay that he was going to help him with a few more opportunities and that was it. The fucking mentorship was over.

Well, Jay didn't need him. The only thing he was grateful for, was him introducing him to Alex. But even then, without Amir, someway he would have found her. It could have taken years, with several obstacles, but soulmates always found each other.

He headed downstairs and poured for himself a full glass of wine. Some 1800 wine, and drank in victory. Amir was not recovering from this shit. He was going to get worse and worse, and then he would die, and Alex would be a widow. In a few months, she was going to move on. With him of course. He toasted to the future before getting a refill.

*

Alex had to take the back entrance into the hospital with how crowded the entrance was with cameras. On the ride over, she had listened to the news, one of which had confirmed that Amir Sheldon had been rushed to the hospital.

Chris was waiting for her, and she apologized for being unreachable. She must have mistakenly switched off her phone.

"How's he? What did the doctor say?" Alex asked worriedly. She was so scared for Amir. He had complained of headaches, nausea and tiredness, but they hadn't taken the symptoms seriously.

"The doctors are still running tests, but you know Amir, he's gonna beat it. He's a tough cookie," Chris smiled.

His words made her stronger. Indeed, Amir was a tough cookie. He was determined and could get through anything.

She waited almost an hour before a doctor finally spoke to her.

"Your husband is physically drained," Dr. Cameron said. "He needs a lot of rest, and will be hospitalized for a couple of days, while we watch him and run more tests."

"But what exactly is wrong with him?" Chris asked.

"We can't say for now, that's why we are running more tests. He's stable now, and if there are any changes we will notify you. By tomorrow we should get the results," the doctor said.

"But he's gonna be okay?" Alex asked.

"He will be."

She went in to see him. His eyes blinked open and he flashed her a weak smile. She stood by his side, staring at him. Why had she not noticed how much he had lost weight? Or how old he was getting? She should have known he was working too hard and was getting close to a breakdown.

"How do you feel? Stupid question I know," she said with a chuckle.

"I feel like shit. Doctor said it could be exhaustion, but I feel differently. I feel drained. I feel... I feel terrible," Amir said. He had never felt this way in his life. Weak in every part of his body. Although the doctor was positive that this was just exhaustion, he was scared that it wasn't. He had broken down in the past, but this was different. He was getting weaker, and the IV was not making him feel better. It seemed like it was making him worse, but it was too soon to make such a premise.

"You're gonna be okay, hun. By next week you will be back home. And soon back to work," she added with a look which told him she was going to make sure he never overworked himself again. She took his hand and he felt better in that instant.

These past months they had been strangers, and truth be told he didn't know why. He barely got to see her, and when he did, they just didn't connect like they used to. Fear made him not ask what was wrong between them again, because he was scared the cracks would lead to an even bigger hole. He had missed her so much.

"I love you babe, a lot," Amir said, squeezing her hand with the little strength he had left.

Tears welled in her eyes at his words. This man indeed loved her. And what had she done? She shoved back the tears and guilt instantly. This was not the time to break down, she needed to focus on Amir and getting him back on his feet.

"I love you too. Now, you're gonna be okay," she said reassuringly.

He nodded in reply, but he doubted so. With how he felt, he had a feeling he was not going to be fine anytime soon.

*

It was late in the night when Alex got home. She had wanted to spend the night but Amir insisted she went home and got some rest. She would return the following morning. She had received a lot of calls asking about Amir's health, and she had left most unattended to, not having the stamina to deal with them. His publicist would put out a report tomorrow stating that Amir had suffered from exhaustion, but he was going to be fine. When she was well rested she would return the calls, most of whom were curious callers who wanted to know firsthand what was happening with Amir.

"Jay?" Alex was surprised to see him in the living room when she walked in. "What... what are you doing here?" He was supposed to be long gone.

"I couldn't leave, knowing what is happening with Amir," Jay said, hugging her.

"You should have left. I could have returned with him, or with someone else," Alex scolded. She wasn't comfortable having him around. She wanted him far away.

"So, you don't want me around?" Jay asked. "Don't worry, I'll head out." He grabbed his jacket and was on his way to the backdoor.

"Jay!" Alex's voice stopped him. "I'm sorry. I just... I was surprised to see you, and I am so stressed out." She hugged him from behind, basking in his warmth. She had certainly not expected today to end like this. It had gone from a 10 to a 0 real quick.

"How... how is he?" Jay asked.

Alex sighed. "He's gonna be okay. The doctors stabilized him and are running some tests. He's been working too hard, and I'm surprised he's exhausted."

The doctors were not going to find anything. The poison he had used could not be traced unless they knew exactly what they were looking for. It was broken down in the body and eliminated in the waste immediately. Amir was not going to be okay. He was stabilized. For now. But in a few days, his health would worsen so fast, and in a few more he would be dead.

"You need to get some rest. You look damn tired," Jay observed, as she covered a yawn.

"Yes I am. So tired. What I need right now is a warm bath," Alex said, as he led her upstairs.

She had the warm bath prepared by Jay, who threw in an erotic massage that gave her more orgasms than she could count. As she lay in his arms, the last thing she thought about was her husband.

CHAPTER FOURTEEN

The aroma of freshly brewed coffee woke Alex up. She turned in bed for a moment, then her eyes opened, staring right at Jay who held a tray. He had made breakfast.

"Jay?"

He grinned as he placed the tray on the bed, giving her a morning kiss.

"This looks great," Alex said, eying the tray filled with bacon, pancakes, and scrambled eggs, as well as her morning boost of coffee served the way she loved it. Dark. "You spoil me so much," Alex smiled, shoving a mouthful of eggs in.

"I would do anything for you. Anything," Jay said, caressing her face.

The past three days, Jay had spent the night over. She had instructed the house staff not to come around. As much as she trusted them, they also had loyalty to Amir, and well, she wouldn't be surprised if they turned out to be those who reveal her business. Plus having Jay around was great for her wellbeing, both mental and physical. When she returned from the hospital drained as hospitals tended to do to her, he welcomed her with warm hugs, kisses, hands and of course his hot dick.

"What are your plans for today?" Jay asked as she finished breakfast.

"First I have to drop some documents at the office, then get to the hospital. Amir should be coming home soon, if they don't find anything wrong with him," Alex sighed. While he recuperated, it would be too risky to have Jay around. Which was why she was taking advantage of these moments they had.

"Have the doctors cleared him?" Jay frowned.

"Not yet. I couldn't speak to the doctor yesterday because he was in a meeting. I'm concerned about Amir. He didn't look great yesterday." He had been unable to talk to her clearly, and she doubted he was recovering, even though he had been stable for a few days. "What are you going to do?" Alex asked as she pulled him gently to the bed.

"I think I'm going to head home, get a change of clothes and..."

His words trailed, as she pushed down his shorts and wrapped her fingers around his member and sucked him almost into submission. Before he could release his load, she grabbed a condom and rolled it over his growing cock.

"Thanks for breakfast," Alex said as her wetness hovered above his manhood.

"Alexxx, you teasing me. Put that dick in you," Alex groaned as he grabbed her hips. However, she hovered above him, writhing against him. He growled, smacking her ass, and getting a scream from her.

As much as she wanted to, she couldn't continue on with the torture, she sat on him allowing his hardness to enter. The both of them moaned in unison. She loved riding him, it made her feel so full. And it gave her control as she got to choose how slow or fast she wanted to fuck him.

"Move that ass," Jay growled as he pulled her deeper into him.

The pace of her breathing increased as she rode his monster dick. The tempo started out slow with his palms circling her nipples. Then he grabbed her hips and pushed her harder onto her, meeting her as she rode his cock faster. She was such a beautiful sight, with her erect dark nipples, her stomach toned. Every piece of her was divine, and he would never forget her this way. Wild and uninhibited. It was only with him she could come alive. Only with him!

He grabbed her ass and flipped her over, thrusting his cock deeper into her. He hated the condom. He couldn't wait to screw her raw, to feel his hot rod as it slammed into her tight box with no resistance between them. He had pleaded with her several times to let him go in raw, but she remained adamant, out of respect to the almost dead husband. If everything went as he planned, his day of going in raw were in the near future. He groaned as he came close to releasing his load, but he needed her to cum first.

Her cries filled the room as she came, clawing at his back with her sharp fingers. He let go of his seed, staring into her beautiful eyes, basking in the intimacy of the moment.

"Now, that was an amazing breakfast," Jay smiled.

*

An hour later, Alex was at her office dropping some documents that needed to be mailed. However, she ended up spending an hour more resolving some office issues that made her decide she needed to either get new employees or fire her office manager. In addition to being an actress,

Alex had diversified, taking advantage of the brand she had created as a result of her fame. She had a real estate company and a charity. She had plans to diversify into the beauty industry and research was being done to usher her in.

Her phone rang as she finally headed out to the car, to go to the hospital. She frowned as she stared at the number. She couldn't recognize it.

"Hello?" she said, getting into the car.

"This is Doctor Cameron, Mrs. Sheldon, you need to come to the hospital. This is very urgent."

"What is happening? Is Amir okay?" she asked, her hands shaking.

"I will explain when you get here," the doctor said.

She had no idea how she got to the hospital with how fast she drove. It was a surprise she was not pulled over. She was consumed by thoughts. What was wrong with Amir? Had they found something incurable in the tests?

She shuddered to think of Amir having some horrible disease as she stepped out of her car in the parking lot, hurrying towards the hospital. She wouldn't think of the worse. However, whatever it was, together they would beat it.

"Mrs. Sheldon!" Doctor Cameron said as she hurried towards him.

"What is wrong with my husband?" Alex asked.

"Your husband is in a coma."

The hallway faded away at the words. She stood there in a dazed state, unable to comprehend what he had just said.

"Mrs. Sheldon?"

She snapped out of the state as the doctor patted her. "What the hell did you just say?" Alex yelled, earning glances from a passersby.

"Mrs. Sheldon, please be calm. I called you as soon as I could. Your husband is in a coma," the doctor repeated.

"But... but... he was doing fine!"

"He wasn't recovering as we expected him to. Remember we assumed he was suffering from exhaustion. But this morning, shortly before we called you, we had a code red. He could not breath, we had to put him on a ventilator," Doctor Cameron continued.

"Oh my God!" Alex burst into tears. "Is he... Is he going to die?"

The doctor sighed. "The test results came out. His internal organs are failing. He's in a lot of pain, and we had no other option than to induce a coma."

"What are you saying? That he's..."

"Mrs. Sheldon, your husband is on the brink of death, but I assure you that we are doing all we can to save him."

Alex was weak. She sat in the lobby for almost an hour in a dazed state, too stunned to believe what she had just been told. Amir was dying. It was unbelievable. Her husband. The man she loved was going to die, and the doctors had still not figured out what was wrong with him.

She hurried to see him. Tears filled her eyes as she stared at him, hooked to different machines, his eyes shut. When she saw him yesterday, had that been the last time she would talk to him? Had that been goodbye? She couldn't contain the tears anymore and wept. She remained by Amir's side until later in the evening and had to be ushered out by a nurse before she left the hospital.

She called Amir's close friends on the way home. She trusted the doctor to keep the news quiet, but when it involved a celebrity, there was usually a leak. Their friends needed to hear from her first before false news began to circulate.

In a few words, she told them what was going on. She was met with shocked silence on most calls. Like her, they had thought it was exhaustion, and that Amir would be back on his feet kicking.

How had her life changed from her having a loving and caring husband, to now having a dying husband? Never, in a hundred years would she have seen this coming. And worse, it seemed like a joke, because she could not fully understand what was happening.

Kim was the first to arrive, and she hugged her tight as Alex cried in her arms. "It is going to be okay," Kim said. But they both knew it was a lie. How was it going to be okay when Amir was dying? He couldn't even breathe on his own.

For the first time, Keisha left her bitchy attitude at home. She wore a solemn look, geared up in black as if someone had died. "He ain't gonna die. I think my husband would die before yours, so be rest assured," Keisha said.

Alex wished she was right. The whole situation was crazy for her. Her husband wasn't even dead, and her friends were more or less consoling her. Their presence did help, but when they were gone, she sat on the patio, staring out into the night.

She loved Amir. A lot. More than she had even realized. He was a friend and a lover. He was an awesome man despite his flaws. It was difficult to find a man like him. A man who cared for her and put her interests before his. A man who loved her despite her inability to give him children, which was cherished by most men. He was the best man she had ever dated. Why couldn't she just have her happy ending?

A tear slid down her face and her body quivered in dispair. She couldn't lose him. She couldn't lose her best friend and husband. It would kill her if he died. She had never thought of death or divorcing him. Her future had always had him in it. She couldn't imagine one without him. They had similar dreams. They had both come from average backgrounds and worked their way to the top. How would life be without him? Cold and desolate.

She reflected on the past months. They had grown so distant, and she was responsible for it. She took a long sip from her wine glass. Just this morning, she'd had great sex with Jay. Probably at the same time he had fallen into a coma. She had hurt her husband. She had made a huge mistake by being involved with Jay.

Although she had a soft spot for Jay, things with him had just been physical. Pure amazing sex. She laughed at how foolish she had been to even entertain his pleas to her to leave her husband. She had been crazy to ponder on it for even a moment. The life Jay promised her were illusions. It was a life built on nothing but sex. And sex wasn't enough to make her love or stay with a man. The man she loved and had always loved was Amir. Amir at the brink of death had opened her eyes to see what her relationship was with Jay. It wouldn't have lasted any longer, as eventually the chemistry would fade away.

"How could I have been so stupid?" Alex wondered aloud. How could she have broken Amir's trust in her by having an affair? There was no doubt she had enjoyed what she had with Jay. It had been a breath of fresh air. It was exciting and new. It had made her feel born again, as for once she had let loose her inhibitions and felt absolute pleasure. Yet, it had not been fair to Amir. He had always trusted her and had been open with her. He had always wanted them to work on their marriage. She should have reached out to him. She should have opened up. There was so much she wished she had done. But it was too late.

Her phone buzzed and she stared at the screen. It was Jay calling. He had called earlier while she was at the hospital and when she returned home, he had called so many times that she had to send him a message, telling him not to come over because her friends were around. She didn't want him here tonight. She couldn't even imagine him in her bed when her husband was in a coma.

Sexing Jay was a mistake, one she regretted now, but she was going to end it. Alex reached for her phone to call him, but changed her mind. She would send him a text instead. He was bound to argue and try to talk her out of it, and she had no energy for any of that drama.

Alex closed her eyes and took a deep breath as the cold night breeze greeted her. She had never felt so alone as she did in that moment. It was dawning on her how lonely her life would be without Amir. In five years, he had become an integral part of her life. He had kept her in check, he had motivated and supported her when she felt like quitting. He had been more than she even realized.

"Please don't die," she whispered into the night, as she hoped for a miracle that would save her husband.

CHAPTER FIFTEEN

Alex was not answering his calls. She had sent him an incoherent message he could not understand. Something about her needing space or shit like that. But he just didn't understand. What the hell did she need space for? Her husband was gonna be dead in two weeks max.

Although it hadn't been confirmed, there were rumors that Amir was brain dead. Messages had been coming in from Amir's fans and other celebrities who were saddened by his state. However, no official statement had been released. He had sent a text to Alex asking about Amir's state, but she had not replied. What the hell was wrong with her? Why was she pushing him away?

He was supposed to be by her side, holding her hand through all this shit. This was why he was her man. However, he wasn't going to let her deal with this alone. He wouldn't let grief make her push him away.

The front door opened and Alex walked in with a grocery bag. She froze in surprise as she stared at Jay, who got up from the couch and walked towards her.

"Jay! You scared the heck out of me! What the hell are you doing here?" Alex said, her heart racing so fast, she was scared it would pop from a heart attack. She had definitely not expected to walk into her front door and find someone, nevertheless Jay.

"How are you?" Jay asked, hugging her, and the grocery bag.

She pulled away from him, walking to the kitchen where she dropped the groceries. He followed her.

"I'm fine Jay, thanks for asking," Alex said.

"I have missed you," Jay smiled, shortening the distance between them. Five days, that was how long it had been since he last saw her. The only time he got to see her was on entertainment news when the media caught pictures of her entering or leaving the hospital. Alone. She shouldn't be doing this alone. She needed a man to be her support. Moreover, Jay had accomplished his mission so he needed to come in before Alex arrived to dispose of whatever was left in Amir's cognac bottle. To his surprise, it was already empty.

"Jay, we need to talk," Alex said, stepping away before he could kiss her.

"What should I help you with? Picking the coffin? Funeral plans?" Jay asked.

She turned to him in disbelief. "Jay! My husband is not dead!" she shrieked.

"But... but the news said he's brain dead. And how am I supposed to know when you don't give me any update?" Jay snapped.

That still didn't give him the right to be insensitive. "Amir is not dead," she repeated for assurance.

"But he's in a delicate state," Jay said. She was having a difficult time accepting the truth, but she needed to. Amir was going to die. And there was nothing anyone could do to stop it.

She didn't say a word. These past days had been torture for her, with her spending all her time by Amir's side. In a coma, he was getting worse, edging closer to death. There was just no improvement on his health. The doctors were confused with all of this, and didn't even know what to do. She had called in specialists but they couldn't figure out what had triggered all of this in the first place. However, she had not given up hope. Another doctor, Doctor Karl, had been flown in from Brazil where he had been vacationing before she reached out to him to help.

"Jay, we are done," Alex simply said. She had thought her text to him had made that clear. Notwithstanding, he should have figured out that things had changed with Amir in the hospital. It was as clear as day.

Jay frowned in confusion. "What do you mean?"

Alex sighed. She really didn't have the patience for this. She was tired. She was drained. "Jay, I mean we are done. This fling, whatever it was, we are done. I'm not fucking with you anymore."

He grabbed her arm as she walked past him, pulling her back. She glared at him. "You are joking right?" Jay asked in a tiny voice he could not believe was his.

"No, I am not. I mean it Jay, what we had is over. My husband is dying, and I realize how foolish I was to get involved in you. Whatever happened between us is over."

He stared at her in surprise, then he laughed robustly. She was joking right? Of course she was messing with him. There's no way she could break up with him. Yeah, she had to damn be joking. Because it just wasn't possible.

"I'm serious Jay, I'm not joking," Alex said. She really should have ended the affair months ago.

"You are joking!" Jay yelled, slamming his fist on the counter top causing the wine chiller to rock.

Alex took a step back, frantically looking around for something she could use to defend herself. This was certainly not a reaction she had expected.

"You are fucking joking! You can't be done with me! You are my woman! My woman! That's a fact! You are my woman!" Jay snapped. What the hell was wrong with her? This was the opportunity they had both been waiting for. For Amir to be out of the way, and she was being a bitch about it? Hell no!

"Is there someone else? Some other man you are screwing?" he accused with narrowed eyes.

"What? Of course not! Stop talking crazy!" Alex said. Dealing with him was definitely more than enough. To have another affair? Please.

He calmed down at this. "I'm sorry Alex... I just... I just..." Of course, she wouldn't cheat on him. She wasn't that kind of woman. Besides there was no time for that. She was always with him.

"Jay, you need to calm down," Alex said. She had never seen him this riled up, and it scared the shit out of her. It was becoming clear he had really thought of a future with her for real. She had figured he was trying to be sweet and all that. Had he really thought she was going to leave her husband for him? Come on! She had thought he was just being corny.

"I'm not calming down Alex, because you are mine. I know you're stressed and I am going to blame this on that.

You are going to think this over and realize you were wrong. And we're going to have dinner together tomorrow night. Understand?"

Alex nodded. As much as she wanted to yell at him to get with the program, her instincts told her to go with the flow so he would leave. There was no need upsetting him more.

Her body stilled as he hugged her, pressing a kiss on her lips. How on earth had she found his kisses attractive? She wondered. Now the kisses repulsed her.

"So, I will go now, but we're going to talk. I will call you later," Jay smiled, as he edged towards the back door.

Alex counted from one to twenty before reaching for her phone, to make sure he had left and was not outside. Then she went and locked the kitchen door from the inside. The first call she made was to a locksmith. She needed him to come over in ten minutes or sooner. The next call was to her service provider, she needed a new phone number. Then she called a private security company she had used a couple of times and had proved effective. She was putting them on her payroll from that very moment.

She didn't know what was up with Jay, and to be honest she didn't give a shit. A lot was going on in her life, and the last thing she cared about was some overfed baby. She never should have gotten involved with him in the first place. She should have realized that he was too damn young, both in age and emotionally.

Minutes later, the new locks were installed, all over the house, as well as the back gate. There's no way anyone was going to get in with those old keys. As the locksmith left, security arrived. She had always been comfortable in her home, with the security cameras barely used. This was not just about Jay, with Amir in the hospital, there was going to be a lot of snooping by reporters and fans. A couple of them had converged at the front gate with gifts and flowers. And while it was caring of them, there were always those ones who could turn violent or wanted to take advantage of the situation. Hence, this was a way to keep the daring ones away.

As she lay in bed at night, she could not help but marvel at the irony of life. About a month ago, she had two men in her life, her husband and then her side piece. The side piece was gone, and so was her husband. Life had played a freakin' game with her.

*

The next morning, Alex was at the hospital as usual. This had turned into her daily routine.

The cameras outside irked her. Couldn't they just let them be? Instead, they were eager to get juicy exclusives of what was happening. What she needed was some peace, instead of the speculating going around about Amir being brain dead, even though it was close to the truth. More calls had been coming in, but she had directed them to her assistant.

Alex had tried to answer a few, and with the kind words that poured in, about how awesome Amir was, she didn't want to be so emotional and break down. Amir had touched more lives than she could count. He was such a humble man, who had given his all into making his community a better place. With almost everyone he interacted with, he created a good lasting impression. She had gotten calls from people she didn't even know he had helped. Black students, college graduates, entrepreneurs, musicians – they all had good things to say about him, how he had helped them or encouraged them to achieve success. She had married a good man. She had always known this, but she had let the knowledge evade her.

She sat beside him on the bed, staring at his face. She missed him so much. She missed those eyes staring at her with love. She missed how beautiful he looked when he laughed. She missed his hugs which always comforted her.

"I'm sorry Amir. I'm so sorry... I..." she blinked back the tears in her eyes as she took his hand, caressing it.

"I miss you so much, babe. So much it terrifies me, of what I would be without you. A part of me feels responsible for this. I feel like this is a punishment from God, for my sin. All these years, I never cheated and you never were sick. And the moment I do, you're deathly ill." The guilt that overwhelmed her in the recent days crushed her. There was always a price to pay, and God had taken him away from her because of her infidelity. How could she have forgotten her marriage vows she made before man and God? Why did God have to punish her this way? Instead of hurting Amir, he should have just dealt with her directly.

"Amir, don't die. I don't know what I would do if you die. Be alive for me. Be alive for the children we are going to have. I promise you I will never hurt you again. Never. I have already cut ties with Jay. What we had... it was a mistake. And I am so sorry. Please, live for me," Alex sobbed, dabbing her eyes with a handkerchief. There was so much she wanted to say. She wanted to tell him how much she loved him. How he meant the world to her. But she was broken. Seeing him in such a delicate state overwhelmed her with grief.

Her phone rang. It was her assistant, Ashley. Alex needed to come over to the office for an appointment.

"Can't it wait? I am with Amir," Alex said with irritation.

"It is Mr. Gomez," Ashley said, referring to a donor to her charity.

"Oh, okay, I will be there in a few minutes," Alex said, ending the call. She kissed Amir on the lips. "Stay strong, my love," she said, resisting the urge to cry as she left.

The moment the door closed Amir's eyes opened.

*

Amir slowly reached for the doctor's call button. It took everything in him to remain still during Alex's confession. His body ached from being on the bed for days. Seven days he had been in a coma. The door opened as Doctor Cameron walked in.

"I am definitely looking at a miracle, Mr. Shelton. How are you feeling? I heard I just missed Mrs. Sheldon. I'm sure she's ecstatic about your recovery," the doctor said.

Although he was still weak, Amir had come out of the coma in the early hours of the morning. The Doctors were so impressed by his ability to breathe on his own so the ventilator was turned down to its lowest setting. The new experimental drugs given to him were working in getting him back from death's door.

"Need a favor from you, Doc," Amir managed to whisper.

"And what may that be?" Doctor Cameron asked.

"No one, including my wife should know that I have come out of the coma," Amir said.

Surprise covered the doctor's face. He had definitely not been expecting such a request. "But... But..."

"Yes, doctor?" He didn't want to believe what Alex had said, he would like to blame it on him still being ill and drifting in and out of sleep while she was talking. That damn kid and his wife? Yet, he didn't have enough. Enough for him to know the whole truth. And the only way he would know the truth was by playing unconscious, giving Alex the opportunity to tell him more.

"You understand me, doctor? No one must know the truth, aside from the other doctors and few other nurses. It is not going to be long." Amir coughed, clearing his dry throat then continued. "A week maximum, I just... I just need to know something," Amir said. It had taken him all the patience he could summon to not reveal to Alex that he was awake. When she had come in, he had wanted to open his eyes, but something he could not explain had kept him still. Perhaps it was the naughty side of him, which had wanted to prank her. Whatever it was, it had aided him in hearing her incomplete confession. And now he needed to know everything.

The doctor sighed. "I understand, Mr. Sheldon. We will keep it a secret, but remember you are a celebrity, and this won't go on for much longer until it leaks out."

"Just make sure no one else gets to know of my state. Thanks," Amir said, reclined on the bed in deep thoughts.

He had been in a coma for about a week now. This was the longest he had ever been in a hospital. The last time was when he was twenty-one and had his appendix operated on, lasting for five days. The doctor said he was a lucky dude. He had stopped breathing and had to rely on a ventilator then too. That was the first time he had been close to leaving this life.

It was incredible how he had gone from being healthy, eating and living right, to being so weak he couldn't get up from the bed. But he was alive! However, he had returned to a different world. Alex had been in a broken state, the worse he had ever seen her, and as much as he wanted to reassure her that he was alright, he needed to know everything that had gone on between her and Jay. He wished he had been able to remain awake to hear it all.

He just didn't want to believe that Alex had sex with Jay. How? So Jay is not gay? It suddenly dawned on him how naïve he had been to think that Jay had been after him. No. The bastard had been after his wife. Now it all made sense. It had been so clear why Jay kept popping around his home, but he had been too blind to see things for the way they were.

It hurt him that Alex would cheat on him. How could she descend so low? To break their marriage vows? It just… it was unbelievable. They had been distant these past months, but never would he have suspected it was because of an affair. Yes, he was pretty sure she had fantasies of other men, even if she denied it. But to go as far as cheating on physically? He had never thought her capable. And with Jay? Come on! Jay was a kid! What had she been thinking? What couldn't they resolve that had made her go that far?

He blinked back the tears that seeped through his eyes. He was a wounded man. He was broken with the knowledge of his wife's infidelity, from her very own mouth. He knew their marriage had not been perfect, but he had certainly not expected it to turn out this way.

Amir wanted to be positive, until he got the full gist, but he knew deep in his heart that was the truth. Alex had cheated on him.

CHAPTER SIXTEEN

Getting into the hospital was easier than Jay had expected. There were a few guards but none paid him any attention as he made his way in. He headed for the restroom and changed into the scrubs he had gotten off Ebay. He knew he would not be allowed to see Amir unless he was on the guest list, and had to get in another way, as a doctor. So, he had done his research on the hospital. He knew the hallways, and he knew the floor where celebrities were usually kept.

The first rule of disguise was to look people in the eyes, instead of looking away with a guilty look. This made you confident, and not appear suspicious so people wouldn't confront you. He strode with confidence into the elevator which took him to the top floor.

Jay didn't even know why he was here. Perhaps he was just too pissed with all that was going on, he needed to see that Amir was almost gone for good. Even in death, he was still fighting for Alex. Damn, Amir.

Because of him, Alex had pushed him away. She had changed her number, and he couldn't get through to her. He had even called her office to talk to her, but they hadn't put his call through to her. And then he had gone over to the house, only to realize that the back gate keys had been changed. His fingers curled in a fist, thinking about it. How could she treat him this way? Like he was a criminal or something? She had pushed him away just like that, after all they had been through. His thoughts of scaling the fence had dived when he noticed the guards on duty. She thought she could push him away with all these attempts but she was dead wrong. They were meant for each other, and nothing could push them apart. The only thing in their way was Amir, who was taking too long to die.

There was only one nurse at the reception desk and she was on the phone, with just a glance at him, with her attention back to her phone. He checked the board in the nurse's station, and saw Amir's room number.

The hallway was quiet, as he made his way to Amir's room. Why was he here again? To gloat? To see for himself that he was close to death? It was like a criminal returning to the crime scene.

The door creaked softly as he walked into the room. He whistled. The luxury money could buy. This was certainly not the type of room he had spent days in when he had fallen ill a couple of years ago. This damn room even had a view. What money could buy. However, money could not buy Amir's life. It was gone for good.

He stood in front of the bed, then chuckled at the miserable state Amir was in. How the mighty had fallen. Once, Amir was full of shit, and had the most gorgeous woman in the world by his side, and now he was just a second away from being six feet under.

"Damn Amir, you look like shit," Jay laughed. "Fucking damn shit! I love this look on you. No more fucking tuxedos, or Rolexes, huh? None of that shit." Jay peered out the window at the view of the manmade lake with swans floating in it. "You gone man, you fucking gone. I don't see why Alex keeps on coming here. There's nothing here for her. You dead bro, dead. Just one pull of the plug and you're fucking gone. And Alex will be mine."

Amir wanted to punch the bastard in the face when he mentioned Alex. Yet, he stayed put. He had come to realize that patience was a virtue. If he wasn't an actor who had played still for years in several roles, he would have easily given himself away.

Jay sat beside the older man, basking in how frail he looked. "I don't know what she ever saw in you. You got nothing to offer her. And you nothing but embarrass yourself every time you try to please her, always leaving that fine woman unsatisfied." He grinned as memories flooded back of them together. "She got the best pussy ever you, know? Tight and sweet. And those breasts of hers? When they bounce... Fucking feel like heaven when I drive my cock into her. We fucked everywhere in your house. Well, except your office. I wanted to, but she refused." He frowned. He should have insisted, but Alex said it was a sign of disrespect and violated Amir's personal space.

"You know I fucked her in the ass? Ate that ass while I fucked her pussy with a vibrator? Shit! There's nothing we didn't do. I know her body well. I can navigate it in the dark." He chuckled at his lame joke. But it was true. He knew every inch of her. He had his touch stamped on it, making her his.

"I gave her what you couldn't give her. Pleasure. I made her cum so many times. Something you couldn't do. You don't qualify to be her man! I do! I know her deepest fantasies. I know how much she loves her boobs sucked. I know she's scared of being tied up, but it still makes her cum hard. I know every freaking thing about her. That she loves to ride dick because it makes her feel in control. But you fucking know none of that!" He took a deep breath. He wasn't get riled up because of Amir. But he was pissed that Alex had ignored him, for Amir.

"When you die, she's gonna be mine. There's no doubt about that shit. Because I have given her everything she wants, and you have given her nothing but money. You don't know that woman like I do. You know nothing!" He leaned forward and whispered in Amir's ears, "You are gonna die, and I'm going to fuck your woman in your office."

There was a noise and Jay froze. It was time for him to leave. He wanted to gloat more. To tell Amir stories of every time, with every detail of how he fucked his woman. But that would be for another day. He ran into a doctor on the way out, quickly making his way down the hallway.

"Who was that?" Doctor Cameron asked. In all his years at the hospital, he had never seen the man. He reached for his phone to call security.

"Don't," Amir said, opening his eyes.

"Are you okay?" the doctor asked.

There was so much pain in Amir's eyes. Every word Jay had said wounded him, replaying in his thoughts over and over. His fear had been confirmed. Alex had slept with Jay. Not one time. Not two times. Not even three times! They had a full fledge-affair!

It was a hard pill to swallow, as images built in his head with what Jay had said. He couldn't connect what Jay said with the woman he was married to. Such wild fantasies didn't seem like Alex. But he knew, there were times he stared into her eyes and saw a wildness. She had hidden that wildness from him. And he fucking was pissed! How many times had he asked her of her fantasies. And she always played dumb! Always played naïve! And yet she had allowed that kid, whose face he wished he had smashed, to touch her.

He gritted his teeth at the thought of his hands on her body. Him driving his dick into his woman! He was going to kill somebody. His fingers clenched into a fist- in rage!

"Mr. Sheldon, please you need to calm down, your blood pressure is rising," the doctor said, observing the EKG machine.

"I'm going to kill that bastard! I swear!" Amir cursed. He was going to wring his neck like a fucking chicken. How dare they? He had trusted Alex to obey their vows, just like he had done. Of all people, she had to go with that prick? Come on! She didn't see someone else to mess around with?

"Mr. Sheldon, please calm down," the doctor repeated.

"I'm going to pay that asshole back. Big time," Amir promised. The bastard had the guts to come in here and gloat. He was pretty sure he was going to die, and he was going to have Alex. The nerve of him! He had the audacity to stand before him in scrubs with his penniless ass and mediocre talents! Amir was infuriated with Alex for making a mockery of him.

If she wasn't satisfied with their sexual life, she should have told him. She had every opportunity to do during their monthly check-ups, or hell she should have just outright told him. He would have changed for her. The things she wanted... he had never engaged in them before. The woman he knew was docile, but she had a side to her he had never seen. But he was wrong. There were times she had been unable to hide them. Times he had gotten a glimpse of that wild woman. Like the time he had woken up to his hands tied up on valentine day. That had been some of the best sex of his life, and he had thought it was a special treat. He should have known. But how the hell should he have known when she didn't tell him?

His marriage was built on secrets. And those secrets had caused cracks in his marriage. Cheating was normal in Atlanta, but he had never expected it would happen in theirs. Everyone looked at them as the perfect and exemplary couple, but the foundation of their marriage had been shaky from the onset.

"Is there something I can help you with?" Doctor Cameron asked.

Amir frowned. He had a suspicion. A crazy one! There had been so much bitterness in Jay. Hate and evil. One reason he hadn't gotten up from the bed to punch him was because he had feared for his life. With how weak he was, Jay would have beaten his ass. Or worse, killed him and walked away. Jay was so convinced that he was going to die, and he wanted to know why. And there was only one way to find out.

"Yes, as a matter of fact."

"And what is that?" the doctor asked.

"More than one favor actually. I need quite a few. First, I need this room bugged with recording devices," Amir said.

The doctor's eyes widened at the request, but there was no doubt it was going to be accepted. After all, what the patient wanted, he got it. Especially, a VIP.

CHAPTER SEVENTEEN

Alex was a shadow of herself. She didn't care about how she looked. What she ate. All she cared about was Amir. She had been clinging on to hope that God would save her husband. Funny how you run back to God after the devil has had his way with you.

"Mrs. Sheldon?" the doctor called.

She burst into the tears she couldn't hold in anymore. With all the money she had, she couldn't save her husband's life. The best specialist in Atlanta had attended to Amir and had given her the gloomy news. Amir was not going to survive. It was only a matter of days before his body couldn't take the stress anymore and shut down completely.

"We need to get someone else to take a look at him," Alex said as she dabbed her eyes with the tissue the doctor gave her.

"Doctor Karl is the best specialist in Atlanta," Doctor Cameron said.

"I don't care! My husband is not going to die. He won't die. He won't," she repeated.

"Ma'am, I understand that—"

"You don't understand anything! You don't! He shouldn't die. Amir has a lot ahead of him. He shouldn't die." Alex was going hysterical. These past days, she was a shadow of herself. She couldn't comprehend what was going on. She was just so tired. She needed some support otherwise she was going to break down.

"Mrs. Sheldon is there anyone I can call to come support you?" Doctor Cameron asked.

Alex immediately thought of Kim, the one friend who always supported her.

Kim was there in less than thirty minutes and she drove her home. Alex had taken a private limo to the hospital as she was too distraught to drive. All during the ride Alex felt numb, looking out the window. She just needed a break. Some time away from all of this.

"I don't know what I am going to do," Alex said as Kim handed her a cup of hot cocoa. "I never thought he would die. I never imagined a life without him. You know it is just so crazy how much I miss him. The man has always been in my life but I never valued him as much as I now do. I guess that saying is true. You know the one about not knowing what you have until it's gone."

"I don't think anything I can say will make you feel better," Kim said honestly. "But I want you to know that I will always be here for you. For anything. You don't have to go through this alone. I will be by your side. All the way."

"Thank you," Alex said. There was so much she wanted to tell Kim. About how strained her marriage with Amir had been. About the affair. But she was too drained to voice her truth, or perhaps she just wasn't ready to let it all out.

Someone at the hospital had said something because the following morning the phone was ringing off the hook. The headlines varied but they all shared the same news. Amir was at the brink of death, and nothing could be done. Kim, who had slept over, handled most of the call, while Alex hid in her room. She couldn't deal with the ruckus happening downstairs. She couldn't listen to the consolation messages trooping in. They came from a place of support and love, but they only upset her. Amir was not dead. Even if the specialists had given up on his case, she believed in miracles. She had committed Amir into the hands of God, and she was hoping that He would intervene, even if it was at the last minute. She had knelt, and surrendered all to Him, confessing her sins to Him, that He should not take out her punishment on Amir. If there was anyone who needed to suffer for her actions, it was her, not Amir who was innocent.

There was a knock on the door and Kim peeked in. She was holding the phone. "It is the mayor, he wants to personally talk to you," Kim said.

Alex really didn't want to talk to anyone. But Mayor Henderson was a family friend and he had reached out to her from the moment Amir was taken to the hospital.

"Mayor Henderson," Alex said.

"What do you need Alex?" the Mayor asked.

"I don't know. All that is happening is so crazy," Alex admitted, choking back a sob.

"If there's anything you need, please do not hesitate to reach out to me. I am more than a leader, I am a friend," the Mayor said.

The calls kept on coming in all through the day, and she had to tell her assistant to come over to work with Kim. The blinds were down in her room, as she lay in the darkness. She just wanted to be left alone. Hell, she wished she was far away from all of this. The bed felt large and empty, and she stared at the side Amir usually occupied.

She found herself in his closet, running her fingers through his clothes. She pulled his robe, and sniffed it, basking in the leftover scent. Tears began to roll down her face.

"I miss you, Amir. A lot," she sobbed. She really hadn't realized how much she loved Amir. They had their differences, but she cared a lot about him. She wanted to give him children be it through surrogacy or other means. She just wanted to spend the rest of her life with a man she loved, and who loved her deeply in return. But she was never going to have that, would she?

It was in the early hours of the morning that she fell asleep, her dreams invaded by one person, Amir.

In the afternoon, Alex headed to the hospital. Her eyes were puffy from crying all night, and well the lack of sleep. The entrance to the hospital was filled with reporters, and she had to go in through the back. Why couldn't they just let her be? Leave her to mourn in peace? But could she blame them? Amir had touched their lives in one way or another, and they were going to miss him as well.

The nurses flashed her kind smiles as she made the way to Amir's room. She stood in the doorway, just staring at him. Every day, she came here and spoke to him. And it sounded crazy, but it was as if he could hear her. There was some theory that people in a coma could actually recognize the voice of loved ones, and this helped them recuperate. It seemed that wasn't happening in Amir's case.

"How are you doing love?" Alex asked, pecking him on the head. "It is so crazy out there. Your fans have mounted a camp at the gates. You are loved Amir, always know it. You came into this world, and you left your mark, for which I will always be grateful. You know it is freaking hard accepting this shit, I don't think I can ever understand it. I just…" She had told herself she was not going to cry today, but there was no way she could hold up that promise. How was she supposed to have a dry eye seeing her husband in this state?

The door opened and the doctor came in.

"Doctor Cameron, I—" Her eyes widened in surprise as she stared at Jay. "What the hell are you doing here, Jay?" she snapped. "And dressed in… in that?" He was dressed in scrubs like a doctor.

"I came to see you," Jay shrugged. He had been following her for the past week. She came every day to the hospital, to be by the side of the man who didn't give a shit about her. A man who was going to die very soon.

"Jay," Alex took a deep breath. "I need you to leave right now. I don't know why you are here. You are not supposed to be here. You are not even on the visitors' list. You are not a family member or a friend. I don't want you here Jay, so leave!"

He didn't leave. He just stood there, staring at her. This was very uncomfortable, even more with him wearing scrubs. It meant he could just breeze in here without anyone being aware. How did he even know that she was here?

"Have you been following me, Jay? How did you know I was... Never mind! I don't care. I just want you to leave."

He pulled her back before she could get to the door, holding her firmly she couldn't budge.

"Let me go, Jay!" Alex glared. He was scaring the hell out of her.

"Let you go? You have treated me badly Alex. Very bad. You changed your number. You changed your locks. You have pushed me away. Why Alex? Why?"

"Jay, I told you we are over. We are done, so stop disrupting my life." She squealed as his grip on her grew firmer.

"We are not done! Amir is dead—"

"He's not dead!" Alex sneered as she pulled herself from his grip, rubbing her arm.

"Look at him. Why are you wasting your time? He's gone already. All that's left is his body. Now, we can be together, you and I," Jay said, taking a step towards her.

"Jay! You need to get that fantasy out of your head?" Was he still stuck on that stupid fantasy? Come on! What the hell was even wrong with him? He was not a teenager for heaven's sake. He was a man! "Jay, what we had was a fling. Nothing more. A fling which was a mistake, which I regret!" she threw at him.

He gripped her shoulders before she could move away from him, pinning her to the wall.

"Don't call our love, a fling! I love you, Alex. I have loved you from the first moment I set my eyes on you!" he snapped.

"Jay, let go of me," Alex said, both pleading and pissed at the same time.

"I'm not letting go of you, Alex. You are mine. You have always been mine. The only obstacle between us was Amir and now he's gone," Jay relented.

"No, Jay. There has never been an obstacle between us. I was never going to leave Amir for you. Never." She winced as he gripped her harder but she kept on talking. "I love my husband. I never told you I would leave him, and I never would have. What we had was a fling—"

"No! What we had was love!" Jay yelled.

"No! It wasn't. It was a fling. It was a mistake!" Alex snapped.

"Don't say that! Don't call me a fling. I know your body, every inch of it. I made you cum. Every time! Something your weakling of a husband couldn't do."

The slap struck his face as Alex yelled at him, "Don't ever call my husband a weakling! Things may not have been "the best" my marriage, but my husband is more than you can ever be! You are dumb ass ever to think I would leave my husband for you!" she laughed hysterically. "Even if Amir dies, there's no way I am going to be with you. Hell no! You are such a child!" She pushed him away. She had been patient with him, but not anymore. She wasn't going to deal with his drama, not now when she was in a such messed up state. Not now when her husband's life was dangling before her.

Alex took a deep breath to compose herself. "I need you to leave now, Jay," she said reaching for the door. She didn't want his presence to upset Amir in any way. She turned around. "What the hell are you doing?" She hurried over and stopped him as he reached for the ventilator. "Are you crazy?" she asked, pushing his hand away. "Are you fucking crazy!" she glared at him in rage.

"Yes! I am crazy for you! For you Alex! You are the air I breathe! You are my everything!" Jay said. He was deeply hurt by her harsh words, but they were coming from a place of frustration with all that was happening. She loved him just as much as he loved her. He wouldn't believe otherwise.

Alex was emotionally exhausted. "No, you don't love me. This is an infatuation and you need to snap out of it real quick. Go be with somebody your age. You have placed me on a fucking pedestal, like some queen and I'm not one...at least not yours. And I don't love you. So get the hell out of here, Jay. Now!"

Jay smiled and her blood turned cold. He looked sinister, and she saw something in his eyes that terrified her. Sleeping with him had been the worst mistake of her life. "I am going to turn off the ventilator," Jay said quietly.

"You are crazy Jay! You are fucking crazy," Alex said, as she slowly moved in front of the ventilator.

"I will Alex, I will turn off that ventilator and you know what that means. But I can spare him if you kiss me, if you be with me, I can spare him," Jay threatened. He didn't want to be cruel to her, but she had given him no choice. If she cared so much about Amir, then she would give into his demands. He didn't care if he had her through coercion, all that mattered was that she was with him.

"You are crazy Jay! What the hell is wrong with you?" Alex snapped.

He spread his arms in a welcome. "I'm not joking Alex. I'm going to pull the plug if you don't be with me," Jay said.

Alex shook her head. She wasn't going to give into his blackmail. That would be the beginning of the end. "I will tell you just like I have told you. Jay, I don't give a shit about you. What we had was purely physical. It never would have lasted. We are done! Understand it? And if you hurt Amir, you will not go to jail because I swear I will kill you," she threatened.

Jay went cold. She had chosen Amir over him? He loved this woman! And yet she didn't care about him the way he cared for her. He stared at her in hatred. She had made use of him, and had now tossed him aside. "You have no idea what I am capable of Alex. You think I am joking but I'm not. It is because I poisoned him that he's there, and I will do far worse. My efforts are not going to be for nothing."

Alex stiffened in disbelief. Surely, she hadn't just heard him right. "What the hell did you just say?"

"Nothing," Jay quickly replied, realizing the truth had just slipped out.

"No, don't back out now. I heard what you said! You said you… you poisoned Amir?" She took a step backwards, as fear and anger overwhelmed her. His good looks dissipated. In his place, she saw the monster he had carefully hidden.

"You are out of your mind. I didn't say that shit!" Jay denied.

"I heard what you said, Jay! You did this to Amir! Oh my God!" Tears pooled in her eyes at the realization. She was the reason Amir was going to die! Her actions had literally killed her husband.

"You need to get some rest. You're hearing things," Jay said, nervously edging towards the door.

She shot out of the door after Jay. "Where the fuck are you going? Come back here!" Alex snapped as he ran through the door. Watching Amir race down the hall, she returned back to Amir's side and burst into tears.

"I'm so sorry, Amir. I swear, I am. Because of me you are going to die. If only I wasn't so stupid. If only I had been honest with you, and opened up to you about what the hell I wanted, you wouldn't be here." Alex was never going to forgive herself. She was going to be haunted for the rest of her life. She had no idea how Jay had done it, how he had poisoned Amir, but somehow he had. She had allowed that devil into her home with open arms. And the devil, taking the form of Jay, had destroyed everything.

Tears fell down her face as she wept for her mistakes. This wasn't a mistake she could take back, as much as she wished she could. This was an irreversible mistake that had cost her husband's life. She was as guilty as Jay even if she had not directly poisoned him.

Jay wasn't going to get away scot-free. She didn't care if she was implicated in it. If her name was spread on the papers ruining her reputation. She was going to ensure that Amir got justice, even if it was the last thing she did.

"I promise you Amir, he's going to pay. I messed up big time, I know, but please forgive me. But he's going to pay. He… he did this to you… How could I have been…" She was too weak to say something else. She was angry at herself. She wanted to yell. To call herself names for being stupid.

The door opened and a nurse stepped in. "Mrs. Sheldon is everything okay?" the nurse asked.

"Yes. Is Doctor Cameron around? I need to speak with him," Alex said, wiping her eyes dry.

CHAPTER EIGHTEEN

Despite the food being better than most hospital food, Amir couldn't wait to get the hell out of the there and get some real food. Probably some burger and fries. For now, he would have to do with this mess. His time here was coming to an end.

This afternoon had been complete chaos for him. He admired his restraint. He hadn't budged or revealed his state while his wife and Jay had been in the room. God knew he had been on the edge, willing to get off the bed every time Jay said a word. To grab him and punch him in the face when he grabbed his wife. He had brought the devil himself into his home. All he had wanted to do was help the kid, just as he had helped others. And he had almost been murdered in that attempt.

Amir had no idea how he had been poisoned, but the truth was out even if the punk had denied it. But he had heard him clearly, and so had the doctor when he listened to the recordings. And Jay would have if the experimental drug had not been used on him.

Doctor Cameron interrupted his thoughts. "Your wife wants us to check your system for poison."

"I see," Amir said. He was supposed to be pissed at Alex. Actually, he was damn pissed and disappointed in her for cheating, especially with Jay, yet he still cared for her. She had shown unbelievable strength that made him admire her. How she held herself through this. How she fought for him to stay alive. He wanted to reach out and tell her that he was fine. She was going through hell just seeing him here, and well she did deserve it, for what she had done. If he had ever doubted her love, he didn't anymore. Despite her mistake, Alex loved him.

Others would want a divorce or some time out, but not him. All marriages had conflicts, and theirs had made him realize that she loved him more than he had realized. Acting unconscious sure revealed a lot about people. Their truth. As well as their ugly characteristics.

"Don't you think it is time reveal the truth?" the doctor asked. "We have that man's confession and he can be arrested."

Amir shook his head. The confession was not enough. Jay would simply deny it. He was sly, and one needed to be careful with him. Amir would bet all his money that Jay would find a way to return to Alex. This time to finish the job, then he would go after Amir. The kid was insane. Where the hell had Brenda gotten him from? He would not be surprised if he had slept Brenda to get to work with him. After this, he wasn't going to mentor anyone. He had learned his lessons.

"So, you are going to continue playing dead? This is becoming more difficult to keep under the lid. We had to lie to the mayor about your state, and that doesn't sit well with me or my staff. And eventually, someone's going to leak the truth," the doctor continued.

"I apologize for the inconveniences caused, but seeing this to the end is important. You heard him. The asshole tried to kill me, but what we don't have enough. He's going to be back, and this time around, we're gonna be prepared. Then we will be done with this façade. You have no idea how much I want to get the hell out of here," Amir continued. He couldn't even walk the hallways for fear of someone seeing him. Just being in the room was a bore, and he was on the alert, anticipating the door opening or the bell being rang by the nurses at the reception for him to pretend, if someone not in on the scheme was coming to his room. This was how he always assumed his unconscious position whenever Alex came in.

The doctor sighed. "I can only give you two days. If nothing happens between now and then, then you have to come clean."

Amir nodded. He was pretty sure two days was enough time for Jay to fall into his trap. "Jay," he said the name aloud in disgust. He had tried to help him. Tried to give him opportunities at becoming an actor. To make a name for himself. He scoffed, then laughed. The bastard had stepped on the wrong toes. What he wanted to do was grab him by the neck and pummel his face in.

Amir had a tough side to him, a side many were fortunate not to meet. He was charming, cool, and all that shit, but he could be an asshole. When he had it in for someone, he would go all the way to mess that person up. And Jay was on that list. The scumbag had come into his home and screwed his wife. Not only that, the scumbag had tried to kill him. And it was definitely not just about Alex. He had heard the greed in his voice. Jay wanted his money, every piece of it. If Alex was even foolish to be with him, Jay would have gotten rid of her as well. He was a manipulative son of a bitch who didn't want to pay his dues, but wanted the rewards that came with hard work.

He reached for the folder the private investigator had delivered this morning. On Jay of course. The young man had fucked his way through to get to where he was. The money in his account, on his cards, even the clothes he had on had been bought for him by other's money. He probably had dreams of being a successful actor, but he would never achieve those dreams. He had been rolling in debts, when he met Amir, and of course Alex came into his sight. Records showed Alex had been smart enough not to fund his lifestyle, or perhaps Jay was actually stupid enough to think he was in love with his wife.

Amir chuckled. Yeah, Alex had messed up messing with that bum. But for him to think she would actually leave her husband for him? What had he smoked? It wasn't even about being materialistic, but despite her being a sex addict as he had come to realize, it wasn't enough to sustain Alex. She wanted companionship, she wanted someone on the same mental level as her, and if it wasn't him, it would be someone else, but definitely not a kid like Jay who spent all he had on clothes and shoes, trying to live up for the Gram.

He wasn't exonerating Alex of her actions. She had messed up. Big time. But he also had a role to play. He had placed her on a pedestal and had thought her to be a saint. A good girl who couldn't do wrong. But now he knew better. She was human and filled with flaws. She was insecure, and had a lot she kept under wraps so as not to be judged. That sense of her being perfect in the eyes of others, including him had affected their marriage.

*

I poisoned him. Jay's words had been replaying in her memory since yesterday. Since he scared the shit out of her by coming into Amir's room. Had he been serious? How had he even gotten the opportunity to poison Amir? She would like to believe that Jay had been bluffing, but it made sense. All of a sudden, Amir had started having those headaches and had fallen ill, with the doctors not finding the cause. It definitely sounded like a poisoning had taken place.

Alex was pissed and disappointed in herself at the same time. She was the cause of all of this. If not for her, Amir would be alive and kicking. If not for her, her marriage would be intact. But she had wanted wildness, instead of creating it in her marriage. She had suggested the doctors looked out for poison, hoping it was not too late. But the doctor had given her an awkward look like she was crazy. Besides, there were countless poisons out there, and they needed to know what to look for.

She needed to get the truth out of Jay somehow. She didn't mind if she had to kiss him. She scrunched at how irritated she was with him. Once upon a time, his hands had caressed her body as he sexed her. But now, she felt nothing for him. Nothing but disgust. If he was responsible for Amir's death, she was going to make him pay. She didn't know how, but she would, regardless of if she was pulled down in the process. Amir would get the justice he deserved.

Alex wanted to share this burden with someone. Her family. Her friends. But she was overwhelmed with guilt. They would be shocked to find out that Saint Alexandria who practically had angel wings had not only cheated on her husband with a younger man, but the said man had also poisoned her husband. The first time she decided to mess around, it came back on her in full force. Talk about first timer's curse.

Tomorrow, she would be going with one of the security guards she had employed to the hospital to keep a watch over her husband. If Jay had tried to kill her husband once, he was going to do it again. He ought to be behind bars right now. The sane thing to do was to call the cops, but they wouldn't arrest him on grounds of her suspicions, when she had no evidence. Jay would simply deny all claims, and her face would be spread all over the blogs.

Her phone rang. It was Keisha. Surprisingly, Keisha had become quite caring ever since Amir ended up in the hospital. For the first time she was beginning to see a good side to her. She called and visited to check up on her, and even occasionally sent meals over.

"Hey Keisha," Alex said.

"How are you holding up, girl?"

Alex sighed. "Terrible. I think what makes it worse is the media. I had to unplug the house phone with the calls coming in."

"Damn those vultures, waiting for carcasses to feed on. They are crazy, you know. Some chick from some blog called me last night asking about Amir's state. You know me girl, I let her have it. I think I made her have a nervous breakdown."

Alex laughed. Her friends had been a great support to her, and she was grateful to them.

"Look girl, with all this shit going on, you need a time out. Gonna throw you a party," Keisha said.

"You crazy Keisha. I don't need a party. I just... I just want to be by Amir's side. I don't even know what I am going to do when he's..." She refused to acknowledge that he would soon die. There was nothing else that could be done, save for a miracle. Initially, she had been full of faith, but not anymore. How could she hold on to faith, when her husband was dying? The prayers made by her and others seemed not to be working, and she feared it was because of her infidelity. She had confessed her sins to God, and prayed for him to forgive her and restore her husband. But Amir remained the way he was. With every day that went by, she lost more faith.

"Fine, your loss. I was going to throw you the most lit parties ever. We were all gonna wear white, and have Amir's pictures everywhere. But now that I think of it, kinda creepy. We can get rid of the pictures and"

"I will pass, Keisha. Thanks a lot girl. I really do appreciate it," Alex said, as tears filled her eyes.

Keisha cackled. "Now you're going to make me wanna cry. I will talk to you later hon."

A noise made Alex freeze. She stared at her room door, as her heart pounded. Had Jay managed to make his way through the security and into the house? She grabbed the heavy bedside lamp, holding it to her chest as her heart continued to race. One, two, three, four... Nothing happened. It had probably been her imagination but she needed to be sure. On tiptoes, she walked to the door, and looked out the hallway. It was dead quiet.

She hated her home. How quiet and big it was, with just her. This house was supposed to be shared with a spouse, and children running around. She pushed back the tears that came to her eyes. Perhaps if she and Amir had had a child, the loss she felt would not be so great. At least she would have someone to turn to. But she was alone. All alone.

When all of this was over, she was going to go far away. On a vacation. And when she returned, she was going to get a pet. Or better, **adopt a child. She didn't want to be alone anymore.**

CHAPTER NINETEEN

Jay had to be extra careful. Alex might have informed the security to be on the lookout for him. He could not be caught. Today was going to be his last day sneaking in the hospital, and that was it. An end to Amir.

He stepped out of the closet into the hallway in his usual scrubs. This time around, he had changed his name tag, and even had on a pair of glasses to throw others off. His heart raced with excitement. He could not wait to turn off the ventilator and watch Amir's peaceful death. Damn, he was going to take a video, so he could replay it every night. His competitor would be gone.

Alex had messed with his mind by choosing Amir over him, and he was going to make her pay. He was going to take away what she valued the most just as she had thrown his love back at him. But he still wanted her. Matters of the heart were hard to control. He was going to hurt her, until she paid for how she had treated him. It was only then he would fully accept her back into his life.

No one paid him attention as he got off the elevator onto the special ward. He shook his head at the lack of security, however it was for his own benefit. Jay peeked into the hallway, there was no guard. He guessed Alex didn't believe he would do such a thing. He had almost messed up that day, almost blurted out the full truth in his rage. She couldn't accuse him of killing her husband without being implicated. He chuckled. He was not going down, but if he did, she would too. He would say she had paid him to kill her husband so they would be together.

His heart raced as he opened the room door. It settled for an instance as he saw that Amir was alone. Killing Amir was so damn easy he was a bit disappointed that there was no challenge. Amir was going to be his first kill, but not his first violence. He had done a lot of research online, and had been watching a lot of movies. While some people felt regret in the aftermath, as well as guilt, it would not be the same for him. All he would feel was delight that Amir was dead, and Alex would be miserable.

Jay stared at the remains of Amir. He looked quite healthy for someone who was supposed to be dying. He was supposed to be a bag of bones, such a miserable mess that they would have a closed casket funeral. How the mighty had fallen indeed. Smug Amir with his well and expensive tailored suits, and wristwatches. Soon, he would be reduced to a pile of maggots.

"I hate you," Jay said. "You ride in fancy cars, live in that big house, and get millions of dollars for movies, but more so than that you also have my woman. Not any longer dude. You're going to die, and I'm going to get everything. I might just get rid of Alex too, and get myself some young bitch who I can screw everyday in your office, in your bed." He laughed as he walked towards the head of the bed.

"Am going to make Alex pay for treating me like shit. For choosing you over me. She brought down my pride by choosing a dead man over me. You, who have given her nothing. And as soon as they pronounce you dead, I'm going to step in and be her shoulder to cry on. I'm going to be there for her, and get rid of her later," Jay said. He knew

Alex was going to be stubborn, she might not want him back, but he would do all he could to get her back. Blackmail her that he was going to tell the public about their affair or even tell the cops that she had killed him. Whatever it was, she was going to regret ever playing him.

"I have always wanted what you have. The money, the bitches, the fame, and I will get everything. Thanks dude. Thanks for mentoring me," Jay laughed at his joke.

"Good bye Amir. You came, you saw, and you fucking went," Jay said his parting words, just as he reached for the ventilator. He ripped the tube out of his mouth, the only thing keeping Amir alive.

Nothing happened. Well, Amir didn't gasp for breath or anything. No flatlining beep on the machine's display. That moment, just as he pondered if he the job was complete, the door flew open.

"Put your hands in the air!" one of the policemen said, pointing his gun at Jay.

Jay's eyes widened in surprise. "It's a setup," he mumbled.

"Put your hands up!" the officer repeated.

"Hello, Jay."

Jay gasped as Amir sat up. The shock to his heart almost made him drop dead.

"I... I..." He didn't know what to say. What the hell was going on here? Amir was supposed to be dead. Not... not alive!

"You tricked me!" Jay yelled as he leapt on Amir. He groaned in pain as Amir grabbed him by the neck, pushing him to the wall.

"You piece of shit! I swear I'm going to kill you!" Amir snapped. He really wanted to break the asshole's neck. Beat the shit out of him.

"Mr. Sheldon, please let him go," one of the officers said, behind him.

Amir hesitated. Why should he let him go, when he tried to kill him?

"Mr. Sheldon, please. Let the law handle this," the officer pleaded.

Alex gasped as she walked into the ruckus. The first thing she thought was that Amir was dead. But then why the cops? Her eyes widened as she saw Amir holding Jay against the wall.

"Amir? Amir? Amir you're alive!" she cried as it dawned on her that her husband was standing without any form of support.

As the cops grabbed Jay and handcuffed him, she flew past him to her husband, throwing her arms around him. Amir hugged her back. Tight. She had missed him so much.

"Amir, you're alive. You're alive," she cried, caressing his face. "How... how?" Jay's presence suddenly hit her. "You... you tried to kill Amir?" Alex said slowly realizing he had gone ahead with his threat.

"You set me up!" Jay yelled, struggling against the cuffs.

"You are mine. Mine! You and your husband are going to pay!" Jay continued to yell.

She turned to Amir. Immediately, she could tell that he knew she had cheated on him with Jay. He knew Jay had tried to poison him. He knew a lot of things she wasn't even aware of yet. "I am so sorry Amir, I am so—"

"Alex, don't do this," Amir said, cutting her off.

"Amir please me, I am sorry, I never meant for any of this to happen. I am sorry," Alex said.

"It is okay Alex," Amir placed a finger over her lips. It felt so damn good for all of this charade to be over. And even more to hold her in his arms. He had missed her.

"Let go of me! I know my rights!" Jay yelled as he was pushed out of the room.

Alex burst into tears. She had never felt so much regret as she now did. Amir could have died.

"Alex, I forgive you," Amir said, caressing her face.

She looked at him in surprise. "You forgive me? But I... I and Jay, I cheated, and he tried to kill you."

"Remember what I said?" Amir asked. He knew many would consider him foolish for forgiving his wife. Not only had she cheated, her lover had tried to kill him. It was enough grounds for a divorce, with the public in his support. It was enough for him to walk away. It was normal for a man to cheat, and his wife forgave him. This was expected and seen as a norm. But often not the other way round.

"What did you say?" Alex asked, puzzled about all that was going on. Her marriage was supposed to be over now that Amir knew the truth. Any sane man would file for a divorce, and as much as she wanted her marriage, she would willingly give him his freedom because she had caused him a lot of harm.

"I told you divorce was not an option. No matter what, I would work through it to maintain my marriage," Amir said. He had not been joking when he told her those words. For him, there were no divorces or ex-spouses. He got married once and that was it. Despite the hurdles and obstacles that would come their way, they were going to work through it. He had known there was no perfect partner, but he had been on the outlook for one he could stand the test of time with. And that woman was Alex.

"But... But..." He was adamant about standing by their marriage no matter what, but she had thought his principles would crumble with what had happened.

"There are no buts, Alex. I meant what I said then, and I mean it now. I love you Alex, and I know you love me," Amir said. Her actions these past weeks had made him realize how much she loved him, despite her mistake. "But if I ever see that asshole on the streets, that is if he ever makes bail, I won't be forgiving towards him. I will mess him up real bad, he's going to regret ever being born," Amir added. He looked upon his wife lovingly, "We're going to work on our marriage. We have a lot of issues we have to deal with, but we will go through it together, and also get those children you want and that dog."

Her eyes widened. He had heard all the things she said she would get if he woke up. How long had he been awake? Now she felt so embarrassed.

"Baby, let's make a promise to each other. No matter what life brings, there will be no more entanglements," Amir assured her as he hugged her tight. He had missed her so much. He was definitely glad the charade was over, and he could get the hell out of this hospital.

Alex hugged her husband tightly and released a sigh of relief. "I promise," she said whole-heartedly.

EPILOGUE

Alex moaned as Amir thrust into her wet womanhood. She tugged against the tie wrapped around her wrist but it refused to budge. His lips pressed firmly into her neck as he pounded into her again from behind.

"Amirr," she pleaded, pushing against him. She hated when it tortured her. Damn, she actually did love it because it gave her a shattering orgasm.

"You feel good," Amir groaned, kneading her gorgeous breasts. He knew what she wanted, but he was not going to give it to her. Yet.

"Amir please, please," Alex begged as he hit her pussy slowly again. She wanted him to fuck her hard and fast. That was what she wanted this morning.

Not able to refuse her anymore, he thrust harder into her. Her mouth formed an O as her fingers dug into the sheets.

"Yes, yes, yes," Alex cried, as her eyes squeezed shut with the ecstasy that overcame her body.

He held her shoulders firmly as his rod stiffened in her. He was about to... he groaned as he released in her, his hot seed filling her up. Together, they fell flat on the bed.

"My hands Amir," Alex said, wiggling her tied arms.

He chuckled as he untied the knot, freeing her. She hugged him, kissing his neck.

Sex with Amir had changed. It had gone from decent to super. He had actually demanded that she open up to him. All her sexual fantasies she had told him and they had ticked all of them off the list in the past years. She couldn't believe she had actually thought he would shame her for what she wanted. He did love them, and with all cards on the table, their sexual life had improved drastically.

Counseling had also worked for them. Although they still had their monthly check-ins, they had visited a marriage counselor for almost a year, realizing that they needed a professional third party to help them navigate through their marriage. It had been crazy at first, as well as awkward, but like Amir, she had been determined to fight for her marriage, and commit all to it being a success.

In addition to seeing a marriage counselor, they had also seen a sex counselor, who had helped a lot with helping Amir gain confidence which had greatly affected their sexual lives.

Alex didn't like looking back at the past, but it was inevitable as it had influenced their present. Having an affair with Jay was a mistake that had propelled change into their lives, teaching them valuable lessons, making them realize that they not only loved each other but that they wanted to protect their marriage.

There had been no way to shut down the news from getting to the press after Jay had been arrested. Heck, pictures of Jay wearing handcuffs while being brought out of the hospital had circulated the media for more than a week. Once the connection between Amir and Jay had been made, there had been so many theories. However, neither Amir nor Alex had confirmed any of the rumors circulating around. There had even been one of Amir and Jay being lovers, and another of a threesome between the three of them that had gone rogue.

Their publicists had done a good job of keeping everything under lid and cover. And well, Jay had kept quiet, especially when shown the evidence gathered against him.

However, the trial would have eventually brought everything to light, as evidence of the recordings and their testimonies would have eventually seeped into the public light.

Amir had suggested letting Jay off the hook to protect their privacy, but with the condition of a gag order and Jay going far away. Amir didn't want to see him again, because he would not be held responsible for his actions. However, Alex had insisted that he get punished by the law. As much as she knew she would be crucified by the press, with her name and career affected, she had not cared that much for the repercussions. She had committed the actions, and would accept whatever the consequences were.

However, while awaiting trial, Jay had killed himself. Found in his bathtub with a slit wrist. It came as a shock to everyone. Amir had gotten a call with the news of Jay's death, and no foul play was suspected.

Alex had never expected him to do such a thing. He had been full of life and killing himself was the last thing she would have expected. However, when she thought about it, Jay was a wounded and troubled person, and death might have seemed like his only way out with the evidence against him.

Jay had left a letter behind, written in his blood proclaiming his love for her. In his words, even in death he still loved her. She had gotten rid of the letter immediately, wondering why the cops had bothered handing it to her.

To be sincere, Jay's death had given them a solution to stop their secrets from being released to the public, with the public left to speculate on what had really happened, while the Sheldons worked on their marriage and careers. There were still those theories floating around, which had become firmer with Jay's death, but life had gone on, as new scandals replaced theirs.

*

Seven Years After The Affair

A freshly showered Alex went downstairs. The aroma of pancakes and bacons greeted her as she walked into the kitchen.

"Mom!" Ashley said, with a wide grin.

"How are you sweetie?" Alex hugged her daughter.

"Good mama, Kevin took my teddy," her daughter pouted.

Kevin giggled. Every time she stared at him, she could not help but marvel at how much he was a replica of Amir. They even had the same mannerism. His twin, Ashley however took after their mother.

The twins had been born seven years ago via surrogacy, and they were the greatest gifts Alex and Amir could ask for. They completed them, and made them realize how much they had missed out on being parents. Their children were God sent and a source of immeasurable joy to them. Their children had shown them that despite the wealth and fame, there was more to life.

"Do it again daddy!" Kevin said excitedly as Amir flipped the pancake on the non-stick pan.

Amir chuckled, and obliged his son with another flip. He looked around the table as Alex settled down next to their children. He was grateful for all he had. For being alive. For having Alex as a wife, a woman he loved dearly, and of course their two beautiful children. He had always said he would have a united family, never broken, and years after that resolution he still stood by his words, unshaken by any calamity that would befall them. He had believed and it was going to come to pass.

He placed the heap of pancakes on the table as he slid into the chair. "Let's eat," Amir said, with a wink at his wife.